FutureWork:

Five Rules for a New Game

Tom Payne

Performance Press of Albuquerque

FutureWork:
Five Rules for a New Game

Publisher's Cataloging in Publication Data

Payne, Thomas E.
FutureWork: Five Rules for a New Game

1. Success in business. 2. Employee motivation. 3. Success - psychological aspects

HF 5386.P65 1996 658.3 95-071195
ISBN 0-9627085-6-9 $14.95 Soft Cover

Cover Design: Dave Payne - Hodge Podge Lodge
Cover Photo: Kim Jew Photography Studios

Printed in the United States of America

See page 160 for ordering information.

FutureWork:
Five Rules for a New Game

Also by Tom Payne

A Company of One:
The Power of Independence in the Workplace

From the Inside Out:
How to Create and Survive a Culture of Change

FutureWork

FRAMEWORK

THE TITLE

THE GAME

THE RULES

Rule 3 - Responsibility (82)

Rule 4 - Relationship (102)

Rule 5 - Fun (126)

The Ticket (152)

FutureWork:

Five Rules for a New Game

The Five Rules:

Rule 1- Know what turns you on - Purpose.

Rule 2 - Be convinced you have what it takes - Confidence.

Rule 3 - Look inside first - Responsibility.

Rule 4 - Remember you're not alone - Relationship.

Rule 5 - Enjoy the trip - Fun.

FutureWork:

Five Rules for a New Game

TEARING THE TITLE APART

As a wise woman, Sara Dunkin, once said, "If you have anything of importance to say, for God's sake begin at the end." The "end," the reason this book was written, can be found in the words of the title, so let's begin by tearing the title apart.

- **FutureWork**

FutureWork is not a time; it's not a place; it's not a structure;

FutureWork is a state of mind.

The way our work is organized will change — always has, always will. But in today's work, changes are vastly more rapid and unpatterned. While many of our organizations are downsizing, others are expanding. Some are centralizing, others decentralizing. Teams are the structure du jour in one place; individuals rule at the other. Some places have TQM and reengineering and others no TQM and reengineering.

What the organization does to position itself for success doesn't matter. The truth is we can do little about decisions concerning time, place and structure made by those in power. We'll assume they know what they're doing.

FutureWork is about knowing what we're doing.

FutureWork is how we, the workers, in today's dynamic times must mentally approach our work regardless of time, place or structure.

FutureWork is how we will thrive personally and professionally in whatever environment we find in front of us — not after the year 2000, but from this moment on.

FutureWork is not a time; it's not a place; it's not a structure;

FutureWork is a state of mind.

- ## Five Rules

The Five Rules must be followed to experience all the possibilities of **FutureWork**, and they don't have to be difficult to implement. The Rules are part of what makes us human. We were born with the potential for applying all the Rules discussed, but over the years some Rules desperately needed today were educated out of us, and some just wasted away through lack of use. For example:

The Rule of Purpose was not a major issue for our ancestors in the hunting and gathering societies. If you hunted and gathered, you lived. If you didn't hunt and gather, you died. Simple purpose.

What about today? Our world's not as simple as life or death. Death we seem to understand; it's life that's giving us fits. The choices of how we live our lives are vastly more complicated than they were in past generations. Our purpose is no longer simple. Do we sell sea shells by the seashore or sell floor space in Cyberspace?

Resurrecting and then committing to implementing the Five Rules become paramount to deciding how we will position ourselves to meet the challenges and excitement of **FutureWork.**

We have what it takes; we must take what we have, and use it.

(NOTE: The Five Rules discussed in this book were determined by the following formula:

Thousands X thousands X hundreds = five.

In layman's language that means the thousands of hours I've spent talking to thousands of people in hundreds of organizations led me to the Five Rules listed in the book. I don't believe these are the only rules, but most of us will be in the big employee picnic in the sky before we've perfected these. Implementing the Five Rules puts us well on the road to success in **FutureWork.**)

- **Game**

A game is any defined activity, venture, undertaking or endeavor with specific rules and outcomes to determine successful completion.

Game in the context of this book is the structure of work. (Not in any way to equate our work with a "game" because we all know how serious our work is, don't we?)

FutureWork: Five Rules for a New Game provides the reader with those distinctly human inner qualities basic to accomplishing, valuing and enjoying work, however that work is structured.

Our desire to implement these Rules and the degree to which we choose to implement them are the choices of every one of us facing an uncertain future. But we must remember when our game changes, we must change. When our game changes fundamentally and radically, we must change fundamentally and radically.

We must do what it takes to position ourselves today to be a success, however we choose to define success, in tomorrow's world of work. It's not that we don't have what it takes to make changes; we all do. We just need to go up in the attic of our humanity, go to the trunk marked "Rules," pull out, and dust off what we need.

WORDS TO READ BY

Ray Bradbury, the author, wrote on rescuing a hummingbird from the jaws of a cat: "I held the bird in my hands, one hand cupped over the other. I could feel the weight of the bird, and would not have known it was there or even alive except I could feel its heart beating. So it is with a good story or a poem. You should feel the heart beat, without feeling the weight of what you are reading."

Elmore Leonard, when asked about the secret of writing his action novels said, "I leave out the parts people skip."

Hopefully you will find **FutureWork** to be written with the heart beat left in and the parts people skip left out.

FUTUREWORK:

FIVE RULES FOR A NEW GAME

FutureWork:

A state of mind

The Five Rules:

Rule 1 - Know what turns you on - Purpose.

Rule 2 - Be convinced you have what it takes - Confidence.

Rule 3 - Look inside first - Responsibility.

Rule 4 - Remember you're not alone - Relationship.

Rule 5 - Enjoy the trip - Fun.

A New Game:

However our tomorrow's work is structured.

THE

GAME

History of the game—

FARMS TO FACTORIES TO FARMS:

A RETURN TO TOMORROW

Once upon a time we, the human race, didn't have jobs. There was plenty of work to be done; we just didn't have the "job" context in which it was done.

We didn't hear conversations like:

> "Grog, what do you do for a living?"
>
> "Well, now I hunt saber tooth tigers; I used to be a fire starter, but I quit that. Too much night work."
>
> or
>
> "Farmer Jones, what do you do?"
>
> "I plant and harvest corn; that's my job."

When things needed to be done, we did them. We gathered, grew and hunted our food, made clothes, threw rocks at drooling animals and etched pictures on the wall. We were busy; our work had meaning and purpose– survival.

We lived with the biological beat of our world. The tides, sun and seasons along with the rhythms of our bodies guided us on our daily adventures. Sure, times were tough, but it has been determined that hunting and gathering societies only spent 15 to 20 hours per week "working." You can bet the subject of "balance of life" was not often bandied about the campfire.

Catching, killing or making

As civilization evolved, when we felt we needed something more than the basics, we caught it, killed it or made it. If that wasn't possible, we used our "free" time and worked for someone else who would "pay" us in some fashion. We'd buy or barter for what we wanted. Then it was back to catching, killing or making.

Why would we want to work for more than we needed?

But the early days of working for wages differed significantly from what we now think of as wage earning. When we first started working for others, we were more like the independent contractor of today. We supplied our own tools of the trade. We were in charge of our own work. We even had a jump on the current rage, self-directed work teams. We hired and fired our helpers. Medical and dental insurance were ideas whose time had not yet come.

But that game was about to change. Between 1880 and 1930, the 20th century corporations were born.

In the beginning, business, as we knew it, was not complicated. You had the big guy (and it almost always was a guy) and the workers, no middle management to speak of. For example in the mid to late 1800s, the Post Office had almost 1700 post offices throughout the country managed by a post master general, three assistant post masters and a few clerks.

Why would we want to work for more than we needed?

Then railroads and the steel industry emerged. Their size, geography and multifaceted operations created middle management and the field's friend, the staff (the organization that's always there to help). The days of the worker being treated as an independent contractor faded into the sunset.

Between 1880 and 1920, the U.S. population doubled. (We obviously were not too tired after a day of doing work that needed to be done.) During the same time, the need for factory workers tripled.

To fill the beckoning ranks, young men and women were coaxed off the farms, away from the shops and stables, and introduced to the novel world of "jobs."

Enter wage labor.

Owing our soul to the company store

As other-directed, wage work unfolded, the organization began supplying the tools. People called "supervisors" or "foreman" told us what to do and how to do it. Starting and quitting time was dictated and benefits were bargained for. We owed our soul to the company store — the seeds of security, as we perceive it today, were sown.

The transition from self-directed to other-directed work provided more imagined security, but abandoning self-reliance was not easy, physically or emotionally. Having to do work others thought important, when and how others wanted it done, was thought to be bizarre bordering on unnatural.

The workers didn't take this strange new game lying down. When wedging themselves into a job, the pull between company security and the desire for independence often became too much. Workers felt they had options, and they left — in droves. Ford Motor Company hired 54,000 people over a twelve-month period to maintain 13,000 employees. And when they stayed, they resisted — in droves. In the 20 years between 1880 and 1900, corporations averaged three new strikes per day!

This mobile and rebellious work force created a need for organizations to develop interchangeable employees, and the employees were treated as such. For example, as stated by John Case in an INC. magazine cover story, April 1993, "A Company of Businesspeople:"

- Training was considered a waste of time, as a matter of fact skilled workers were a liability, not an asset. If they left, they were hard to replace.
- Jobs were defined as narrowly as possible. The simpler the task, the easier it was to fill the job.
- Workers needed close, direct supervision.

Ready Freddy

Enter Frederick Taylor.

Frederick Taylor's scientific management pitted workers against the clock. Since many workers had not had much use for a clock with its artificial division of time and were too busy doing their "job" to care, an activity was created for the "keeper of the clock" and added to the manager's job description. More to do meant more managers were needed. Between 1910 and 1920, the worker class grew two and a half times slower than the manager positions.

In 1916, Henri Fayol wrote *Principles of Administration* while running a French coal mine. He defined the role of management as planning, organizing, commanding, coordinating and controlling. Max Webster came to the same conclusion studying the German Army. Thus the role of management as it has been played out for years was defined. (Like a coal mine and the German army, does that explain some management styles?)

Over time we settled into a life with jobs defined by others and directed by managers who planned, organized, commanded, coordinated and controlled. It was the same for all our competitors; so there was little need or desire to change. The company took the place of extended family providing both financial and emotional security.

Our position in our new family was defined by a box on the organization chart. That box contained a title, a description of duties, a salary or wage cap, a career path, a health plan, a pension and social status. If a new requirement was placed on the organization, we drew another box on the chart and filled it with a willing worker — the family grew.

And we all lived happily ever after —— Not!

Back to the Farm

The very conditions producing the concept and necessity of the "job in a box," i.e. the production of things in mass quantities by momentous human effort, began rapidly fading away. Work still needs to be done, but the structure of the work has changed.

Technology drove us to the factories; technology is now driving us away.

The question is, "Are we ready to go back to the farm?"

> **Technology drove us to the factories; technology is now driving us away.**

Are we ready:

- To retrieve the independence skills, those "Rules" that may have withered over the years?

- To recognize, without being told, what work needs to be done and what expertise we have to contribute to that work?

- To give up putting our future into the hands of organizations we do not control?

Are we ready to take back our lives?

Today's game differs from the game of our ancestors in a very vital way; we can now remain at the factory and work as if we're on the farm. We can, and must, be "self-employed" while working for somebody else. Work needs to be done whether we do it from inside the organization or from outside. Where we physically are (mail stop 34A79 or in the spare bedroom at 20 Shady Lane) is not important. What we do is important, not where we do it.

In yesterday's game, the popular technology made use of our bodies; today's technological game uses our minds. Because of our intellectual competencies and our desire to use them, we, the employees, control the primary factor of production, and we can function as effectively in or out of the core organization.

Let's carry our farm and factory metaphor a little further and look at a couple of ways to view the emerging relationship with our jobs.

Feed the dog

What is the major benefit of the factory? The answer is one word, SECURITY — as demonstrated by wages, benefits, social structure and consistency. The down side of the factory is that this security comes at a heavy price. That price is the lack of CONTROL — the control over work, time, finances and future.

Sure, the above is a generalization, but, I believe, a pretty accurate one. Whatever our feelings are about the factory, we must realize how quickly the factory game is changing for each of us.

Warren Bennis, author and professor at the University of Southern California, said, "The factory of the future will have only two employees, a man and a dog. The man will be there to feed the dog. The dog will be there to keep the man from touching the equipment."

Like it or not, reality is being fired at us point blank. All jobs are temporary — always were and always will be—-but there will always be work.

We don't have to just "feed the dog." The challenge is there for each of us to position ourselves by resurrecting those skills and abilities that are core to success in this changing world of work — the Rules of a New Game.

Was it more painful to be dragged kicking and screaming into the factories of yesterday or dragged kicking and screaming out of the factories of today?

Considering we homo sapiens have been working on this earth for more than 50,000 years and for only one hundred of those years have we worked in factories, shouldn't we be genetically better equipped to work on the "farm" — to work independently?

Implementing the state of mind that is **FutureWork**, either inside or outside the organization, will enable us to find the only true source of security — the self-respect we will feel doing work that is meaningful to us and acting on our own hopes and dreams, not somebody else's.

Farms to factories to farms.
Independence to dependence to independence.
We've played the game before, and we can play it again.

All the struggle to learn and all we have to do is remember.
East Indian saying

What game are we playing?

REALITY

Before we can successfully get to where we want to be, it's essential we know what game we're playing — not the game we'd like to play, not the game we think we should be playing, but the game we ARE playing. Reality.

> **Like it or not, reality is being fired at us point blank. All jobs are temporary - always were and always will be - but there will always be work.**

What is the current state of the farm and of the factory?

Fruits or motor home

As was once said "Good advice usually works best when preceded by a bad scare." Before we emerge into the 21st century, ponder this sobering thought concerning today's organizational reality.

YOUR ORGANIZATION DOESN'T CARE WHAT YOU THINK!!

While you're sitting nice and comfortably, reading this book, people who don't even know you are making decisions that will affect your future, making decisions that will change the way you thought your tomorrow would be.

That's reality.

What percentage of employees in your organization were asked for input to the organization's future strategic plans, including downsizing, reengineering, consolidation, etc.?

As they say, "The truth shall set you free, but first it will make you miserable." The company doesn't care what individual employees think! I repeat this reality because if we don't get it, there would be no incentive for anyone to work on the Rules of a New Game.

Organizations care about what the employee body as a whole thinks and what the unions think. Not caring wouldn't be good business. But your organization doesn't care specifically about what any one individual (you, for example) thinks!

So we may be strolling through life with a vision of working for three decades, reaching the age of an elder, being compensated handsomely by the organization to which we gave the bulk of our youth then cruising off into the sunset in our motor home to be nurtured by the fruits of our life long labor.

This vision may run headlong into an organization's vision, an organization making decisions without our fruits or motor home in mind. We feel betrayed.

Clear vision, mucky reality.

A difference in ages

I was born in 1940. The reason I divulge that "so what" factoid is that research has determined people's belief systems are formed in approximately the first seven to ten years of life. Basically those folks born between 1940 and 1949 tend to view the world differently than do those born between 1960 and 1969.

When I started my first corporate job, I firmly believed that if I showed up on time, got an average or better performance rating, and didn't lie, cheat or steal, my company was going to keep me employed.

What do young people hired right out of school today think about the longevity of their jobs? While giving a dollar's worth of effort for a dollar's pay, many view their jobs as stepping stones, places to learn about the industry and to network, all the while faithfully looking for what's next.

So when a rumor of possible organizational downsizing occurs and processes through the "They owe me a job" belief system, how is that person feeling? How about the person with "I was looking for a job when I found this one and I'll find another one" belief? Same downsizing, different results — based not on the downsizing itself, but on what is believed about the downsizing game.

Is the game you're playing helping or hurting you?

Why

I won't bore you with statistics, because I'm sure I can bore you without statistics. We're all aware of the millions of jobs that have been restructured out of existence over the last decade.

Tom Peters' book, *The Tom Peters Seminars: Crazy Times Call for Crazy Organizations*, describes a work world beyond current imagination. He suggests we eliminate the word, "change," from our vocabulary and substitute "abandonment" or "revolution" instead.

Why all of this abandonment and revolution?

Downsizing started out as a legitimate reaction to competition and the economy. Even the most bitter of us would have to agree many of the organizations of a decade ago could have used the organizational equivalent of Jenny Craig.

Then downsizing became a fad. Ask the likes of General Motors, IBM and Westinghouse. Over a 16 month period (mid 1992 to mid 1993), 29 CEOs were "dehired" because they didn't change fast enough. (Imagine how briskly that message spread through clubhouses and boardrooms.)

What followed was a fixation. The downsizing amounted to corporate bulimia. Layoffs could be a part of the herd mentality or the bandwagon effect. When one organization does it, it becomes more acceptable for others. It's an addiction. (For example, IBM has laid off all the people they can, so they just laid off 1300 people from Westinghouse!) Like a bulimic, organizations may be leaner but not necessarily healthier.

The reality of the reality

A look at what is happening:

◆Downsizing can limit an organization's ability to develop new products, research, advertise and train. This reduction in vital business components can reduce the number of new customers and limit growth which creates the need for, you guessed it, more downsizing. A study by the AMA found that two-thirds of companies downsizing liked it so much they did it again the following year.

◆While "layoffs are a last resort," is often said, research showed less than ten percent of management actually tried pay cuts or shortened work weeks prior to layoffs.

(Why when we talk about rightsizing, does it always means laying somebody off? Ever hear of organizations rightsizing and adding workers?)

◆Three reasons organizations downsize according to Michael McGill in his book, *American Business and the Quick Fix:*

1) Necessity — reduces expenses.
2) Possibility — technology, others doing it.
3) Desirability — closer to customers, faster reactions to market.

◆Think about the interesting situation we, the workers, find ourselves in. If we don't tighten up our processes and maximize our technology, our competition will eat our lunch, and we could lose our jobs. If we do tighten up our processes and maximize our technology, our organizations will not need as many people, and we could — lose our jobs!

(That dilemma reminds me of a Woody Allen line, "More than at any time in history, mankind faces a crossroads. One path leads to despair and utter hopelessness, the other to total extinction. Let us pray we have the wisdom to choose correctly.")

◆Downsizing corrects the mistakes of the past, but it's not designed to create the future. Something else has to do that. And that something else may well be reengineering — that's the good news, but it may also be the bad news considering that the most pessimistic of the prognosticators say that if organizational reengineering is carried to its extreme, we could lose 25 million more jobs.

Jobs lost for non-economic reasons are gone forever.

The blacksmith and the iceman

As if 25 million jobs lost aren't enough to get us to sit up and take notice, consider this reality — jobs lost for non-economic reasons are gone forever. Jobs lost to technology, reengineering a process and the like are gone forever. Ask the blacksmith, the carbon-paper makers, the iceman and radio sound-effects people.

The media says the jobs are coming back, and organizations are hiring at a greater clip than last year. What is not being said is what jobs are coming back. Are they the same jobs that were lost?

According to Price Pritchard in *New Work Habits for a Radically Changing World*, the first functional industrial robot was introduced during the 1960s. By 1982, there were about 32,000 robots being used in the United States. Currently there are more than 20,000,000. When a factory lets go of assembly-line workers because of advanced technology, and we hear that the factory is hiring again, do you think it's to replace those same workers that were let go? Probably not, but somebody has to maintain those multiplying robots.

The reality is, our security does not, and can not, lie with our organizations.

The reality is, our security does not, and can not, lie with our organizations.

If security is not in our organizations, where must it be? Security must be in ourselves, in our abilities and in the quality of our work.

I don't mean to be pessimistic, rather to be realistic and excited as to the source of our security. As David Noer said in his book, *Healing the Wounds: Overcoming the Trauma of Layoffs and Revitalizing Downsized Organizations*, "They (workers) do...have the opportunity to make a real choice, and that may be a once in a life time gift. Breaking organizational co-dependency and taking responsibility for our own work is our ultimate...challenge."

The other side of the coin

As I try hard to emphasize whenever I corner more than two people in a room: if we are not in control of our organization, and we put our security in the hands of our organization, we are then saying we do not have control of our security. A very stressful position to take!

If we are not in control of our organizations, is it in our best interest to be dependent on them?

When I first started writing the book, *A Company of One*, I was thinking about those folks staring straight into the eyes of a downsizing. I quickly discovered a more treacherous side to that coin.

What happens if you are in a downsizing organization, you make the cut but don't like what the organization has become yet don't feel you can leave? Or what happens if you are in a rapidly growing organization which seems to change daily and you do not like what the organization has become, but you don't feel you can leave?

If we don't like what our organization has become, if we don't like its beliefs, values, culture and respect for people, if its new mission does not complement our personal purpose; then for the good of both, we should part company.

Let's look at another reality of modern-day business

Money - Everything else is just helper words

An organization must concentrate on three aspects of the business:

- customers
- employees
- bottom line

(Also there are suppliers, environment and society as a whole but the above are the Big Three.)

When organizations concentrate on customers, customers provide what's required for the bottom line which enables organizations to keep their employees.

Organizations must also concentrate on the employees. Then the employees will be happy, fulfilled, well-trained and committed to serving the customers which will bring in more customers who provide what's required for the bottom line. This concentration enables organizations to keep their employees.

Organizations must concentrate on the bottom line which will allow the organization to provide the highest quality at the lowest cost. This approach will bring in customers who provide what's required for the bottom line which enables organizations to keep their employees.

One, two, three

While organizations must concentrate on all three, they can only FOCUS on one at a time. Where is your organization focusing? If you had to rank (1, 2, or 3) customers/employees/bottom line by order of decision-making priority for your organization right now, how would you rank them?

When this question has been asked in programs, the overwhelming response has been: Bottom line - first, customers - second, and employees - third (or sometimes fourth).

What are organizations doing to get workers to think this way? (Enter here all the "re" words, e.g. realigning, reengineering, restructuring, etc.)

What do you think of that rating? Is it OK for the organization to focus on the bottom line first?

What is the objective of a for-profit business? Here comes another dollop of reality — money. All other words are helper words! And money is all the objective has ever been.

How an organization makes money may vary. Sometimes concentrating on the employee makes money, and sometimes concentrating on the customer does the job. The end result of either of these concentrations is the focus of making money.

As Aldous Huxley said, "Facts do not cease to exist because they are ignored." Fact: If business does not accomplish its bottom line, there will be no customers. Without customers, employees are a real extravagance.

> **If business does not accomplish its bottom line, there will be no customers. Without customers, employees are a real extravagance.**

I was thinking about this the other night when watching TV. What's the mission of NBC? To provide entertaining and educational television programs for their customers, us, the viewing public? I think not. If it were, why do they keep putting their most viewed programs opposite of ABC and CBS's most viewed programs. This little bottom-line-oriented ploy sends all of us "customers" scurrying around to find a blank tape and the instructions for the VCR so we can eventually watch what the networks know we want to watch now. How about airlines with the number of customer/sardines per flight, long lines, and the careful distribution of eight peanuts, is this customer or bottom-line orientation?

If your organization is a not-for-profit or a public-sector entity, you still have a bottom line that drives all decisions. That bottom line is usually thought of as the mission of the organization. But if we think about what ultimately drives the decisions of any organization, it becomes obvious that the not-for-profit or the public-sector organizations are, at their core, driven by the same economic forces as are the IBMs or the Microsofts. If you do not accomplish the bottom line, you're history, and your motor home may be no more than a dream.

So what would you do?

In reality how easy is it for your organization to increase significantly its customer base? Obviously, it's an uphill battle for most in today's changing, competitive and global market. So if your company is having difficulty significantly boosting the customer base to increase the bottom line, what's the alternative? Right, to reduce expenses and what (who) accounts for 50 to 60 percent of organizational expenses — employee salary and benefits.

What would you do if you were responsible to the shareholders and you needed to improve the bottom line right away? Best bet is to reduce the biggest, line-item expense. A true bottom-line orientation has the management aligning with the shareholders. The employees and the customers become costs to contain.

Also considering real estate accounts on average for about 25 percent of the assets of a Fortune 500 company, watch what will happen with the use of office space in the future. (Here comes more of the virtual office.)

If you're financially bottom-line oriented, would you rather pay your workers by the hour or weekly/monthly set salaries? Set salaries are a real bargain in a 60-hour-work-week environment. Watch the future of salary structures.

The reality many organizations now face is that the main benefit to the bottom line of cost cutting may have already been achieved. So to produce more revenue growth, that is to build up the customer base (tough job), we need to do it with a smaller, and in many cases, disillusioned work force! If we are not willing to increase the supply of something, in this case the employee base, then we must increase its yield. And reality is, with the mood of workers today, organizations have a big job ahead of them.

Who does what?

Really, what's the responsibility of an organization? Did the founders of your organization have an idea, garner capital, adhere to all the government regulations, hire a bunch of strangers, negotiate for real estate and experience many sleepless nights all for the purpose of making you happy?

Did they bring their burning desires and passion to life in order to provide strangers long-term financial and emotional security? Was your organization founded to be an extended family, the home away from home, the place to go each day for fulfillment, challenge and an enhanced quality of life?

Maybe the only real responsibility of an organization is to provide a safe place to work and an honest day's wage for an honest day's work. The reality is we, the employees, provide the rest.

Don't get mad, stay even.

I believe getting mad at our organizations for the game they're playing is a waste of valuable energy, getting disappointed, yes, but not angry at what "is." Don't get angry at reality, especially considering if we were king or queen, focusing on the bottom line is what we might also do.

There is the classic story of the scorpion and the frog.

> The scorpion wanted to cross a river, but couldn't swim, so he asked the frog to give him a ride over. The frog said, "No, because you might sting me." The scorpion said, "If I did that we'd both die." This made sense to the frog, so he gave the scorpion a ride. Half way across the river, the scorpion stung the frog. The frog looked up in disbelief and said, "Why did you do that? Now we'll both die." The scorpion said, "It's just my nature."

Reality is, the nature of organizations is to be bottom-line oriented. If the interest of an individual employee runs up against the interest of the bottom line, the employee loses. We can be disappointed if we want, but being angry doesn't pay.

If the interest of an individual employee runs up against the interest of the bottom line, the employee loses.

An interesting article to that point was in the October 3, 1994, Fortune. In a piece on customer service, a story is told of Rosenbluth International, a travel-management company. Hal Rosenbluth, president and CEO, wrote a book entitled, *The Customer Comes Second and Other Secrets of Exceptional Service*. The stated Rosenbluth philosophy is to "hire nice people, treat them well, encourage them to bind emotionally with the company, train them continuously and equip them with the best technology. The customers and profits will follow. "This sounds like employee - first, customer - second, and bottom line - third, doesn't it?

But wait!

The article goes on to say that "this formula worked enormously well, although the company did run into some turbulence this year when the continuing slump in business travel forced it to lay off 217 employees..."

Even when the president and CEO writes an acclaimed book on the importance of the employee, when "turbulence" strikes the bottom line — good-bye employees. Reality!

(Note to organizations: When you're developing your mission statement, if you can't stay in business without a positive bottom line, for gosh sake, say it! Employees know the reality of the situation, and they'll appreciate and bask in the sunshine of your honesty.)

The question each of us must answer is, "Can I thrive in an organization playing a bottom-line orientated game?" If not, and you're in one, what are you going to do about it?

Core/contractual/flexible

This next reality is an original thought of mine. I know it's original, because I originally got it from Charles Handy in his book, *The Age of Unreason*. In this book, Handy sets out the three elements of business: core, contractual and flexible.

- Core

Those jobs without which the company cannot function, i.e. mission essential jobs.

Remember, reengineering carried to its logical conclusion could mean 25 million more lost jobs. What's left after the 25 million jobs disappear is the core.

- Contractual

Folks who enjoy being self-employed or can't find a job in the core.

Self-employed numbers are growing at four times the rate of salaried workers. (Self-employment is not new. In 1900, 50 percent of American workers were self-employed. By 1977, it was down to 7 percent and up to 13 percent by 1993 according to Tom Peters in Excellence Extra Newsletter, June 1993.)

We're in a cycle, farms to factories to farms. Reality!

Individuals are not the only entrants in the contractual segment. Many of our larger business are both core and contractual. They're defining their own core competencies and outsourcing, (i.e. contracting out) much of the remaining activities while at the same time acting on contract for other organizations.

For example, a communications company determines its core competency is being a full service communications company. They do that job better than anybody else (definition of core competency), but they don't maintain buildings better than anybody else. So they outsource building maintenance.

To whom does this communications company outsource building maintenance? They contract with an organization whose core competency is building maintenance. The building maintenance company outsources communications, since it is not their core competency, to — a communications company.

- Flexible

Part-time workers.

Outside of the federal government, Manpower is currently the largest employer in the United States. One-half of the part-time workers have gone this route because they couldn't find full-time employment. Most of the rest love the flexibility. How long before temps outnumber permanent employees? Some say within ten years.

Shift happens

How many people in your organization are occupying a core job? How many are occupying a job that could be contracted out, i.e. outsourced? Almost no job is immune. I heard the other day (a true story) some farmers in Wisconsin were outsourcing cow milking. Why not? There are people whose core competency is cow milking which frees the farmers to do farmer things like applying for government subsidies.

Is it just a coincidence that another way of saying "outsourcing" an activity is saying "farming out" an activity?

> **Is it just a coincidence that another way of saying "outsourcing" an activity is saying "farming out" an activity?**

When American Airlines said it was going to contract out some 550 jobs, an analyst for the airline industry said "What airlines are doing now is remolding themselves into what an airline would be today if it started over again. If you started today with a clean piece of paper, you wouldn't own anything. You'd rent the pilots if you could." Reengineering with outsourcing added!

A real-world example of outsourcing: TopsyTail Company with sales of $80 million, a staff of only three full-time employees and 20 outsourcing vendors who handle everything from manufacturing of hair care products to servicing retail accounts.

Why would organizations choose the Contractual/Flexible route? Why not? With an eye on the bottom line, outsourcing provides a means to remain globally competitive while avoiding an uncertain economy, oppressive employment rules, anti-discrimination laws, sexual harassment issues, health-care costs, pension plans and expensive training. Serious issues for a bottom-line-oriented organization!

Reality check — everyone in the final analysis is in business for him or her self, always was and always will be.

A company of one

Each of us must stop thinking like an employee and start thinking like a *company of one* who's been hired to do work needing to be done. The reality is all employment is temporary. We are all JIT (Just-In-Time) employees. We need to look for work that needs to be done and do it, whether we're in or out of the organization.

William Bridges, author and change consultant, in his book, *JobShift: How to Prosper in a Workplace Without Jobs*, calls the future the "dejobbing" of America. He contends job holders will continue to be eased out of work with the work turned over to people who float from project to project and company to company. People will have assignments, not jobs. Bridges says that in today's fast moving economy, jobs are "a rigid solution to an elastic situation." Bridges' ideas on the future of jobs, require approaching our work with a whole new mind set—**FutureWork**.

My son, Dave, is a film director and screen writer in Hollywood. He explained how a movie normally gets made. The producer develops an idea and pulls in a director. They settle on a writer, actors, acquire some investors and hire a line producer. The line producer hires a director of photography, casting director, art department, production designers, grips, gaffers, transportation people, make-up and special effects, — all those folks whose names roll by while we're leaving the theater.

They combine their talents for a specific amount of time with a single objective. When that objective is complete, i.e. a movie is made, they all go their separate ways looking for other movies to be made. What we have is a team of JIT, *company of ones*, coming together for a finite project. A look at the future?

Reality check — everyone in the final analysis is in business for him or herself, always was and always will be.

My sister-in-law is a project manager for a construction company currently building a hospital. When the building is complete, Joelle is unemployed until she finds another project and another team to join. How many of your friends or family are *companies of one* today? The future is here, and it requires new Rules.

What will outsourcing mean to our standard of living? Reality is that lower skills (maintenance, security) will probably be paid lower wages in an outsourced environment than were paid by big companies. But contracting organizations providing higher skills gain advantage from their lower overhead and greater efficiency, and therefore can afford to pay their workers as well or better than some in-house positions. Also since the market for higher skilled people is good, pay will stay competitive.

In his book, *Moments of Truth*, Jan Carlzon remarks, "If you aren't serving the customer, you better be serving somebody who is." I personally feel if you are in the second group, serving someone who is serving the customer, and you want to remain in the core, you're in trouble. An organization's main thrust as it relates to structure has to be to put the employee in position to directly serve the customer, anybody else is expendable.

If we're not contributing more than we're costing — we're gone.

If we're being paid more than the open market is willing to pay for our skills, then we have a "challenge." If our pay is consistent with the market's willingness to pay for that skill, we can go anywhere!

> **If we're not contributing more than we're costing — we're gone.**

We can't let some of today's uncertainties get us down. Working in the 21st century can be rejuvenating. One small example, with so much of today's work being knowledge work, and with real estate costing what it does, who's to say we have to gather in an office? More of us will work from home, and home can be anywhere we want it to be! Reality!

So what?

Many of us are in organizations that for whatever reason may not have our individual best interest at heart — organizations that are being openly and blatantly true to their bottom-line nature. Because of this reality, we may be driven, or choose to go, from the known of the factory to the unknown of the farms.

So what? We can do it. We have all we need to make the transition smoothly.

To thrive in a game that's changing faster than the metaphors used to describe change, people must resurrect basic human competencies.

We must implement the Rules of a New Game:

Rule 1 - Know what turns you on - Purpose.

Rule 2 - Be convinced you have what it takes - Confidence.

Rule 3 - Look inside first - Responsibility.

Rule 4 - Remember you're not alone - Relationship.

Rule 5 - Enjoy the trip - Fun.

These Five Rules are natural to us all.

We must be conscious of their existence,

convinced of their need,

and committed to their implementation.

THE

RULES

FutureWork:

Five Rules for a New Game

RULE 1 - PURPOSE 

RULE 2 - CONFIDENCE

RULE 3 - RESPONSIBILITY

RULE 4 - RELATIONSHIP

RULE 5 - FUN

The main thing is to
keep the main thing
the main thing.

A bumper sticker

RULE 1

KNOW WHAT TURNS YOU ON

PURPOSE

Purpose is what gives our lives
meaning, passion and energy.
It's our dreams, our desires.
Purpose gets us up at the break
of dawn, possesses us through the day
and well into the night.
It's what makes our daily endeavors exciting;
it turns us on.

MR. FIX-IT

In 1985, my wife Jean and I moved from Chicago to Albuquerque, New Mexico. That was a great year. The next year the kids found us. Our excitement tapered off a bit, but we still knew the Southwest was for us. When we arrived in Albuquerque, we bought a house and had a swimming pool installed.

We had our pool, deck chairs, table and an umbrella, but something was missing — a shelf. We needed a shelf mounted outside of the kitchen window. On that shelf we could put out party items like blue corn chips with salsa and being health nuts, the juice of several marguerita s.

We asked our neighbors for a recommendation for someone to furnish and install the shelf. Their recommendation — Mr. Fix-It. Despite the name, we gave him a call. An appointment was set.

Mr. Fix-It arrived, right on time, and much to my surprise, (the first of many) Mr. Fix-It, the handyman/carpenter was dressed like an English professor. I explained my shelf needs and asked for an estimate.

As we walked around to the backyard, Fix (I felt I knew him well enough by that time to call him by his first name) asked me more questions about how we use a backyard than the real estate agent asked during the entire home-buying process. He took measurements, asked a few more questions and gave me an estimate.

Since I didn't want to seem too easy, I said I'd get back to him with our answer. As a result of his previous probing questions, he got me thinking about other things, like where we were going to store the chemicals, hoses, covers, all the miscellaneous pool paraphernalia. So being really into this spending money thing, I asked him for an estimate on a couple of additional cabinets.

Imagine how a man calling himself a handyman/carpenter might react to that "buying signal." Fix said, "Mr. Payne, you told me you have not enjoyed a summer by your pool as yet, so I would like to make a suggestion. Before you invest additional money in cabinets, spend a summer, use your backyard, use your pool. After you have lived with what you have for a season, if you still feel you would like cabinets, you'll have a better idea of how many and where they would be most conveniently located."

I told him waiting to order sounded perfectly logical (although unexpected from a handyman/carpenter), and we would be getting back to him on the shelf quote.

As we walked to his van, I saw the reason for Mr. Fix-It's rather unconventional behavior. On the side of his van in large letters read: Mr. Fix-It. That, of course, was no surprise, but under the large letters was written the reason Mr. Fix-It showed up exactly on time, the reason he dressed and spoke as he did, the reason he asked the questions he did, the reason he responded to my impulsive request as he did, and the reason I'm telling this story. The entire message read:

Mr. Fix-It Adjustments to Human Environment

Mr. Fix-It didn't see himself as a handyman/carpenter, he saw himself as an "adjuster of human environment" and behaved as someone committed to adjusting human environment would behave. How might he have behaved if on the side of his van were written:

Mr. Fix-It Net $75,000 This Year

Mr. Fix-It knew his purpose, being an adjuster of human environment. If his purpose had been to net $75,000 next year, I would have had cabinets over every square inch of the backyard that wasn't water.

Fix had a purpose and he fulfilled that purpose through his job. His purpose directed how he dealt with himself and all those with whom he came in contact.

Direction in a world with a seeming shortage of direction is what the Rule of Purpose is all about.

PURPOSE: What is it and why is it a Rule?

I don't intend to saddle us with a profound definition of Purpose. Purpose, in the context of a Rule for a New Game, means simply "the reason we exist." (Glad we're not being profound!) Purpose is what gives our lives meaning, passion and energy. It's our dreams, our desires. Purpose gets us up at the break of dawn, possesses us through the day and well into the night. It's what makes our daily endeavors exciting; it turns us on.

The reason Purpose is a Rule is that as workers today we are facing more than Alvin Toffler's *Future Shock*; we're now facing option shock. Without highly structured "jobs" and with technology changing our game by the nanosecond, **FutureWork** is oozing with endless potential.

Taking guidance from our elders and/or suggestions from our mentors about how to live our personal and/or professional lives is increasingly more difficult. Their history need not be our destiny. Tomorrow's a clean slate. We have ourselves a window of opportunity if we just get off dead center. Those clichés aside we, more so than any workers in the last century, are now free to carve out a future we can be genuinely wild about.

> We, more so than any workers in the last century, are now free to carve out a future we can be genuinely wild about.

But with that freedom comes responsibility.

- The responsibility to push ourselves to identify what we want our future to be.
- The responsibility to position ourselves in front of work that excites us.
- The responsibility to know the work we're doing is worth doing.
- The responsibility to know, and to live, our purpose.

When analyzing the work we want to do, remember all work is important if it is consistent with our purpose, not harmful to the community and supportive of the environment.

As the saying goes, "It's easier to ride a horse in the direction it's going." Our work (the horse) is going in a different direction than it has gone in the past — not necessarily a better or worse direction, just different. We now have more options which create a better opportunity than our parents or grandparents ever had to take some positive action by creating a future we can get excited about. We are in control; we are in charge.

REFLECTIONS ON PURPOSE

Vision - The living purpose

Since our discussion of purpose may sound like a discussion of vision, let's examine the difference in how vision and purpose will be used in this book.

Purpose is an essential ingredient for vision. Purpose, as described, is the reason we exist; vision is the manifestation of that purpose. Mr. Fix-It saw himself as an adjuster of human environment (purpose), and that passion manifested itself through him being the owner of a thriving handyman/carpenter business (vision).

A business definition of vision is what a business sees itself as successfully doing in five years. Personal vision is the same, but to insure our vision is desirable and worth fighting for, we must know what turns us on, our purpose.

Survive or thrive

With all of the structural changes in today's organizations, some growing, many downsizing, the only consistent factor is the workers. Organizations (Fortune 500 or sole proprietorships) survive by renting our behaviors, our time, and our physical presence, but organizations thrive when they receive our excitement, devotion and passion.

How many people do you know who in their jobs as they are structured today actually "make" anything? How many of us produce a product or service that goes directly to the end user? How many of us actually see the culmination of our toil? Without that immediate feedback, remaining excited, devoted and full of passion is tough. How easily can a personnel records supervisor of a drug manufacturing company relate to the improved health of a customer she never sees?

People in today's multi-functional, "job-in-a-box" organizations crave the fulfillment of purpose. People in tomorrow's organizations will demand it.

Remember it's important the Rule of Purpose (and the other Rules) is equally vital for both those associated with organizations or those self employed. Either way, the mind set of **FutureWork** requires that we find work consistent with our purpose, wrap our work in passion, and get on with it.

Living by default

We all have a purpose. That's the good news. The not-so-good news is many folks don't know what their purpose is, and the undefined purpose is directing their everyday behavior.

It's imperative we come to our purpose not by default (knowing what it isn't) but by a conscious knowledge (knowing what it is). If we back into purpose, we back into vision.

While knowing what we don't want is a good start, backing into purpose isn't effective in the long term simply because the subconscious mind doesn't focus on the opposite of an idea. For example, if you closed your eyes and tried not to think of a golf ball, what do you think would fill your mind's eye? Sure, a golf ball as big as a domed stadium

How does this help or hurt our pursuit of purpose? How many people do you know who are saying things like, "I don't want to lose this job," or "I don't want to move to Vermont," or "I don't want to have my pay cut." When they close their eyes, all they see is working in a different job, sitting under a maple tree in Vermont making less money. Not a very positive vision!

We need to concentrate on what we really want to have happen. What do we really want? As a kid, did you run around telling all the other kids that when you grew up you wanted to work for the company you are working for now and live in the town you are living in now the rest of your life? Has your current job always been a dream of yours?

What is your vision? Is it your vision to have a house, car, and college tuition for the kids? Are there other ways to get what we want in addition to doing what we currently do for a living? Are there people who have a house, car, and college tuition and don't know the job we're knocking ourselves out performing even exists?

Knowing our purpose, expressing our vision, and concentrating on getting what we really want will open up other paths to achieve what we desire to accomplish. Have you ever walked through an airport and had your name announced on the loudspeaker system? That gets your attention, doesn't it? How aware of the loudspeaker were you before you became the center of attention? We're open to things perceived by us as a value or a threat. Without purpose, how do we know what's a value or a threat?

Living on purpose

Through most of my life, at some level, I envied those folks who really knew their purpose and what work would help them fulfill that purpose, and then pursued that work with reckless abandon.

(I guess maybe that's why we ask little kids what they want to do when they grow up — we're looking for ideas!)

My younger son, Dave, always knew what he was going to do before he even knew you had to "do" anything. He was going to be in the entertainment business. Halloween was his favorite holiday because he could wear costumes and fix the garage into a "spook house." He entered parades so he could dress like a clown and became a teenager for the same reason. He acted in and directed school plays. He played baseball with limited interest in the sport, but sports provided great theater!

Dave, the screenwriter and director, is living his purpose, his vision, his life!

Dave beat the odds. A survey of 1350 of our employed brethren by the Gallup organization found 41 percent of the respondents consciously chose their jobs or careers, 18 percent got started through circumstances, 12 percent took the only job available, and the rest were influenced by friends or relatives. Those numbers mean 59 percent of us workers are worried about losing a job we didn't want in the first place (and might not like much now)!

I was one of the 59 percent. I joined the work world after completing my military service. I took the job with the most secure company offering the most money. So with $132 a week coming in, a wife, a new son and a degree in economics, I started to work as a sales-person. Seventeen years later, I had the same company, same wife, same son plus one, same degree, and, thankfully, a somewhat better salary.

The point is I must have had a purpose, and that purpose drove the vision of working for a secure company, bringing in an acceptable income, enjoying medical and dental insurance, raising a June and Ward Cleaver family in the Chicago suburbs, retiring and dying. That must have been my purpose because all of my behaviors led to that vision.

About thirteen years into working for the company, two very pivotal events occurred in my life. My brother, Bill, invited Jean and me to a Wellness Weekend, a four day workshop put on by the company for which he worked. The weekend dealt with mental and physical wellness. At this program, we were exposed to issues like personal purpose and personal goal setting. These discussions gave me a lot to think about.

Six months later I was transferred within the company from a job that occupied me six days a week, ten hours a day to a job where on some days I had nothing to do. (Send me a SASE for more information.) This job was a perfect set up for a dangerous combination — I now had time to think and something to think about!

Was I doing what I really wanted to do with my life, and if I wasn't doing what I wanted, why was I doing it?

That question led to the realization that of everything I had, all I really wanted was my family. The rest, like the other 59 percent of workers, I just stumbled into.

Some changes needed to be made. I had to give up "purpose by default" and begin to clarify what I did want. This clarification of purpose was important. Since I was making decisions every day about how to spend my earthly time, I might as well spend this valuable time doing what would help me get what I really wanted.

I internally committed to a new future, didn't even write it down, just committed to it at the subconscious level, then went about my everyday business. But my business was never the same again because every decision I made, from the minuscule to the magnificent, was made with clear future in mind. I now have the same family and a whole new life. Purpose driving vision works.

Was I doing what I really wanted with my life, and if I wasn't doing what I wanted, why was I doing it?

Let's take a look at what our purpose might be driving.

COMPONENTS OF PURPOSE

Values

Our purpose is what turns us on; our vision is a revelation of that purpose. Values are the priorities we set to accomplish our purpose.

The having/doing/being trap

An interesting way to focus on our values and how they might be influencing our mental voyage into **FutureWork** comes from a book by Richard Lieder, *The Power of Purpose*. In this book, he talks about the Having — Doing — Being trap.

Having is defined as having "things," i.e. money, house, clothes. *Doing* is what we do to get the money, house and clothes. *Being* is being maximized, living our purpose, experiencing meaning, essence and passion in our lives.

The reason this is described as a "trap" is that many folks' thought processes run along the lines of: if they "have" enough, that will allow them to "do" what they want to do, and they will therefore "be" happy. While that sequence may sound logical (and all too familiar), how many people do you know who bought into that value system who are genuinely happy?

The reason focusing on "having" doesn't work is because we can never have enough. (We may not vocalize our purpose is to "have" but what's our driving force?) If we had everything, where would we put it? Can we ever have enough clothes, enough money, and just the right house?

A Roper poll which didn't need to be conducted concluded: people earning between $10,000 and $30,000 felt they needed between $50,000 and $60,000 to have everything they needed. Those earning $50,000 to $60,000 say they needed $125,000. When we value "having," and we can't ever have enough, we tend to frustrate ourselves. (Maybe we have trouble making our ends meet because our ends are too far apart?)

Do we appreciate everything we have now? If not, why would we want anything more?

How would it be if we reversed the disheartening value system? "Be" who we are; be clear on the real reason we exist, our personal purpose. That will lead us to what we should "do." Then we will "have" everything we need to have. It's a matter of values.

Do we appreciate everything we have now? If not, why would we want anything more?

Gotta have; I ain't getting

If a person is unable to experience "being" on the job, then the subject of "having" takes on additional significance. As Peter Block explored so well in his book, *The Empowered Manager*, the fact some people value "having" so highly gives a good indication of the level of "being" that's experienced on their jobs. Because if trudging off to work each day does not bring personal satisfaction, we want to "have" a lot for the sacrifice we're making.

Why do we think our concern over job security is so great today? Could it be that losing security may negatively affect our "having" and our purpose would be thwarted?

Will we be mentally approaching **FutureWork** with the purpose of "having?" Will we be unsatisfied unless we die with more toys than our neighbor?

Often we blame the company for the pressure we feel, but who is "the company" but a bunch of us coming together to accomplish a specific objective. Let's look at how we view *having/doing/being* affects today's organizational actions.

Would organizations rather have fewer people working longer hours (e.g. ten people working 60 hours), or would they want more people working shorter hours? (e.g. 20 people working 30 hours) If you said ten working 60, you agreed with the majority of people in workshops who work for financially bottom-line-oriented organizations. The 10/60 approach tends to be less expensive in overall overhead.

But what is required to get ten people to put in that kind of a grueling week? People must be willing to do it. The U.S. Department of Labor says the average worker now does the work of 1.3 people and overtime has hit an all time high averaging 4.7 hours per week. And why do they do it? For money! So they can "have" more.

The game we're playing may be creating more of our world than we think.

My older son, Tom, in his early years really put an interesting spin on the "having" value. Grandma gave Tom $2.00 to spend at the Flea Market. The first item he saw that intrigued him was a brand spanking new dollar bill sold at the booth of a coin dealer. Tom liked the looks of the crisp, encased dollar so he bought it for $2.00. As the morning wore on, his fascination with the dollar bill wore thin. When he passed a booth selling toys, he saw a 60 cent squirt gun which looked better to him at that moment than the dollar bill. He used the new dollar bill to buy the 60 cent squirt gun.

Not good business in the financial sense, but in the big-picture sense Tom traded in money which has no value in itself and all day long he had in his possession what to him did have value. Tom, to this day, better than anyone I know, understands the real value of a dollar.

Mission - Organizational Purpose

What purpose is to an individual, mission is to an organization. We've discussed personal purpose; let's discuss organizational mission and examine their relationship.

What do we believe to be the mission of our organization, our work unit, our *company of one*. I know the subject of mission has been beaten to death, but it's like a character in a horror novel who just keeps coming back to life, and rightfully so. As Peter Drucker said, "One of the most important things an organization can do is to determine exactly what business it's in." Or another way to phrase Drucker's statement, "What game are we playing?" Simple stuff, but it's not often being done.

Nothing scientific here, but my experience tells me that 97.857% of today's workers couldn't say what their organization's mission was if their life depended on it. And that's a shame. Because we all have only 168 hours a week in which to do things; we might as well be doing the most effective things.

Once the bureaucracy is gone, organizations are flattened, and workers are empowered, mission may be the only realistic way to insure everyone is pointed in the same direction. To have a work force with motivation pouring out of their ears, but motivated over the wrong thing, is less than useless; it's actually destructive.

The same or not the same, that's the question

How would it be if why you exist (personal purpose) and why your organization exists (organizational mission) were the same reason?

It doesn't get any better than that. You go to work each day, and every moment you spend on the job helps you advance your personal purpose.

How about the opposite extreme? Your organization's mission bears no resemblance to your personal purpose. How does it feel to go to work each day?

I can answer that first hand. When I began the mission/purpose thought process, I was missing a couple of vital components. I was not aware of my organization's mission, nor had I given any thought to my personal purpose.

While working in the telecommunications industry, it hit me I was spending all my working hours giving people dial tone. I began to think "providing dial tone is not what I want to do with my life." I was backing into my purpose. I knew my purpose wasn't dial tone; I just didn't know what it was.

That flawed thinking was never really explored further until I was out of the industry. I wasn't just "providing dial tone;" I was "providing access to a global network which would allow the free flow of vital information." This mission, if I had known then what I know now, was partially compatible with my personal purpose of enhancing individual performance, for myself and others.

Most people don't fall in the extreme (that's why they're called extremes) of complete compatibility or incompatibility with organizational mission and personal purpose. Most of us find ourselves in jobs that allows us to employ at least a portion of our personal purpose.

For example, a woman acquaintance was a marketing director for a large organization. She was not having fun. After a discussion of finding purpose on the job, she made a commitment to become clearer on what her purpose was. She understood it involved journalism which she studied in college and hadn't worked in since.

She cornered her boss and asked if she could write and edit a quarterly newsletter for the field sales force. The boss liked her idea, and while she wasn't given any extra time or money, she was given permission. When last we spoke, she was a much happier and productive person blending to some degree her personal purpose with the organization's sales mission.

My friend found her purpose on her job which is preferable to having to leave the job to find purpose. Staying where you're at is desirable, (especially if you haven't exterminated the "having" bug as yet). Rookies almost always make less money than hardened veterans. So strictly from a "dollars and cents" viewpoint, if "having" is important, stay put. You'll be consistent with your core purpose. Also if you're the kind of person who absorbs praise like a sponge and is a bit leery of the ridicule that may come with failure, think about the challenges a new career may throw at you.

If you can't find the proper blend of mission/purpose in your current job, "having" is on the back burner, and you're looking for new challenges, go for it. For example, a man in a recent workshop was a scientist for a federal agency. A few months after we had talked about some of these issues, he called and said he had quit his job. He and his wife were moving to Kentucky to train race horses.

Life may be short, but it's wide.

If you can't find your personal purpose on your current job, for the good of all concerned, get out. But try for a purpose/mission match before you leave.

A wallet full of money

Did you ever wonder why when people are working on a job they feel is meaningful, worthwhile and "purpose" full, they rarely spend valuable time discussing such mundane "having" issues as pay, working hours, office size, desk location, crowded employee parking lots, or the personal hygiene of coworkers? The answer is these trivial concerns pale in comparison to the perceived importance of the work being done. If this conclusion is true, what does that tell us when we hear people complaining constantly?

> **If you can't find your personal purpose on your current job, for the good of all concerned, get out.**

Some people's excessive concern over issues such as money, working hours and physical environment provide an indication of their level of dissatisfaction with, or lack of knowledge of, the basic meaning or purpose of their work. They don't know how or if they are making a contribution.

If we don't feel our work matters to anyone (including us), we will have an inordinate preoccupation with anything tangible we can squeeze out of the time we're "wasting" at work. If what we are doing at work does not fill our being with passion, it had better fill our wallets with money. The less important we feel inside, the more important we want to seem outside.

We all search for fulfillment somewhere. As George Bernard Shaw's often repeated quote points out, "There is no greater joy in life than to be used for a purpose considered by yourself to be a mighty one." We all have to feel what we do is important, that we are contributing something. If we don't find personal purpose in our chosen line of work, we're going to find it somewhere. When we do, watch out world. We work without counting the hours, and what we earn takes its proper place. We all know the power of being fulfilled by something we do.

How about being fulfilled by what we do for a living?

If what we are doing at work does not fill our being with passion, it had better fill our wallets with money.

Blue Monday, hump day and TGIF

How many people's lives revolve around weekends, vacations, retirement and death? That depressing circle of life is passed along through the "Blue Monday" gene. This "gene" creates a whole new generation of workers spending their days dragging to work on Blue Monday, staggering through Hump Day, and anxiously awaiting TGIF, only to shuffle again to work on Blue Monday completely forgetting what they did on the weekend.

Thanks to this genetic defect, many of us grew up with a clear distinction between work and play. Work is what we have to do, and play is what we want to do. A character in Richard Bach's novel, *Illusions*, said, "The more I want to do something, the less I call it work."

Consider the amount of time we spend physically, mentally and emotionally at our chosen profession. If work is an activity viewed as a "have to" rather than a "want to," unnecessary limitations are placed on our passion and energy. Both personal and organizational productivity are reduced.

(If you agree with the commercial saying, "The best part of waking up is Folgers in your cup," either you should get a more exciting purpose or reassess with whom you're sleeping!)

"We must learn to love what we do or do what we love," according to George Burns. That will happen when we find purpose and passion in our work.

We should all be challenged in the most positive sense about the uncertainty of the future. We don't have to be obligated to do what we've always done if we don't choose to. We can choose in **Future-Work** to work on purpose.

OTHERS' VIEWS ON PURPOSE

☒ John Brodie, ex-professional football quarterback, professional senior golfer and TV broadcaster quoted his wife as saying, "John, you may get to be 65 years old without ever working a day in your life." Did she mean it didn't take work to be a professional football player, golfer and broadcaster? No, she meant he was, heaven forbid, having fun doing what he did for a living. He actually enjoyed it; he was living his purpose. What an interesting concept!

☒ Sammy Davis Jr. played the role of a dying tap dancer in the movie, *Tap*. Sammy's movie daughter was admonishing him for continuing, in a weakened condition, to sneak out with his old cronies and dance. Sammy told her, "If I stop dancing, I'll still be dying. I'll just be bored doing it." Then he spoke the most powerful line in the movie, "I'm a tap dancer." As simple as that line was, it set the priorities of the life of Sammy's character. A dancer was who he was. It was his priority. It was his game. It was his passion. It was his purpose.

☒ While Sammy's character was fictitious, there is the true story of Karl Wallenda. Karl was the founding father of the famous high wire act, the Flying Wallendas. Ten years prior to Karl's "work related" death, he was asked about his feeling for the tightrope. He replied, "Being on the wire is living; everything else is waiting." A wire walker was who Karl was. It was his priority. It was his game. It was his passion. It was his purpose.

☒ Viktor Frankl in *The Unheard Cry for Meaning*, said "The truth is that as the struggle for survival has subsided, the question has emerged: survival for what? Ever more people today have the means to live, but no meaning to live for...Unlike other animals, man is not told by drives and instincts what he must do, and unlike man in former times, he is no longer told by traditions and traditional values what he should do. Now, lacking these directives, he sometimes does not know what he wants to do. The result? Either he does what other people do — which is conformism — or he does what other people want him to do — which is totalitarianism."

☒ Studs Turkel in his book, *Working,* quotes a health care writer, Nora Watson, as saying, "Most of us...have jobs that are too small for our spirit."

☒ In *Wind, Sand and Stars*, Antoine De Saint-Exurpery writes, "The man who sinks his pick axe into the ground wants the stroke to mean something. The convict's stroke is not the same as the prospector's for the obvious reason that the prospector's stroke has meaning; the convict's stroke has none."

☒ Norman Mailer interviewed in the June 15, 1995 American Way magazine said, "As for life being absurd, I think [Jean-Paul] Sartre, despite his immense intelligence, did a disservice with the idea life has no meaning. I don't think life is absurd. I think we're all here for a huge purpose. I think we shrink from the immensity of the purpose we are here for."

☒ On TV's *Sixty Minutes*, the wife of violinist, Yehudi Menuhin, when describing her famous husband stated, "Great music comes out of him." Interviewer, Ed Bradley, asked, "Why?" and she answered, "Because that's what's in him." On another *Sixty Minutes* segment, tennis great, Andre Agassi, was asked about his renewed passion for tennis. He replied he had a "desire to be nowhere else" other than on the tennis court. When at work do you have a desire to be "nowhere else," or would you rather be "anywhere else?"

☒ R. J. Johnson took two years to create and produce a Public Broadcasting System program, "Look Who's Laughing," centering on the life and comedy of six disabled comics. When asked what his next project would be he said, "My rule is I pursue the ideas which won't let me go. They wake me up and talk to me. That's what I'm looking for next."

"...Ideas which won't let me go. They wake me up and talk to me..." That's the heart of the Purpose Rule for success in **FutureWork.**

REALITY OF PURPOSE

If we were to ask our favorite motor club to map us a route from St. Louis, Missouri to Bakersfield, California, they could. If we asked to be routed to Bakersfield from "wherever," we'd have been given that smile reserved for little children and dumb animals. Because in order to get from here to there, we must know two things:

1) What does "there" look like (vision)?

2) What does "here" look like (reality)?

Harold sees his purpose as helping to raise the living standards of underprivileged adults in impoverished areas of the world through improving their education. This purpose creates for him a vision of opening a school in rural Mexico. That's what "there" looks like for Harold.

But Harold has a spouse in ill health, three school-aged children, and an eleventh-grade education. He has never been out of his home state and only knows enough Spanish to order a cerveza in Tijuana. That's what his "here" looks like.

Harold's purpose and vision can still be accomplished. But he'll need to comprehend clearly the current reality of his situation, so he can take the steps necessary to get himself from "here" to Mexico.

All too often in today's spirited times, those fortunate ones who know their purpose and define it in a vision will never arrive because they're oblivious to where they're coming from.

ABC's of reality

If "A" is our current reality, and "B" is our vision, when we remain focused on "B," we'll get "B." If we lose focus and make only a small change ("C"), we'll wind up at "D" wondering how in the heck we got there.

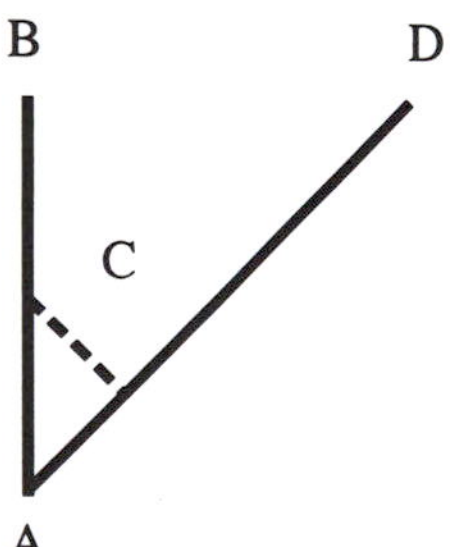

Our lives are full of "C's." To decide if doing a "C" is in our best interest, we must know what turns us on (purpose), what our purpose will look like when we get it (vision), and our starting point (reality).

Much of the frustration I've experienced in the thousands of hours spent with employees is due to the intense desire to ignore reality.

The TV character, Roseanne, said about husband, Dan, who was building a boat in their garage, "You've got to give a man his dreams, so he doesn't realize you control his reality." If others control our reality, how easy will it be for us to accomplish our dreams? If others control "A," wouldn't it be up to them if we ever got to "B?"

Much of the frustration I've experienced in the thousands of hours spent with employees is due to the intense desire to ignore reality.

"A" is "A," but we control what we do with it.

For us to develop our personal purpose and generate a vision that compliments our organizational mission, it's imperative we're clear on just what the heck is going on right in front of our noses. (For a closer look at what's in front of our noses, refer back to Reality.)

SO WHERE DO WE GO FOR PURPOSE?

Religious leaders? Family? Society? Television? Workplace?

No!

Purpose is influenced but isn't created from any outside source; it's our personal hopes and dreams. Purpose is drawn from the inside out.

Questions, questions, questions

➯Here are a few questions which can lead to the formation of a personal purpose statement:

1) a. What should I do (taking into account my education, family, finances, background, etc.)?
   b. What do I want to do?

2) Why am I here?

3) What do I have to contribute that will make a difference?

4) What do I value and believe in?

5) Considering my answers to questions one through four, what seems to be my personal purpose?

6) How can I experience my purpose:
   a. In my personal life?
   b. In my work life?

In our workshop programs, people are given time to answer these questions for themselves. This gift of time is appreciated although strangely not always used. When given one hour to be alone to discover answers by working through the purpose questions, some folks find the time too long. One hour is too long to contemplate what drives every aspect of their lives? How long do those same people spend each day reading the newspaper or watching reruns of "Happy Days?" One of life's frustrating mysteries!

Life partner's purpose

➪If you're in a significant relationship, discussing the above questions with your life partner is powerful. "Why are we together?" Understanding purpose helps us focus our energy on what's important and provides us with the most critical input for decision making. For example, in today's turbulent times, with both parties often working outside the home, if one of the partner's job requires an out-of-state transfer, how do they decide what to do without a clear understanding of personal and mutual purpose?

The answers to these questions are critical. What we are doing externally, individually and/or as a couple, determines our success in the future, and what we do externally comes from the internal belief of purpose.

Get on the stick

➭If you don't have a work unit mission statement, push your boss for it. If you're the boss and don't have one, get on the stick and develop one. If you have a mission statement which is gathering dust under "M" in your file cabinet, resurrect it and make it a major input in your decision making processes.

A mission that excites us determines whether we come to work each day because it's a work day or because it makes a difference.

A mission that excites us determines whether we come to work each day because it's a work day or because it makes a difference.

For more thoughts on purpose, in addition to the books already mentioned, consider reading: *Even Eagles Need a Push* by David McNally (Dell), *I Could Do Anything If I Only Knew What It Was* by Barbara Sher and Barbara Smith (Dell), *The Path of Least Resistance* by Robert Fritz (Fawcett Columbine).

PURPOSE: The short version:

The reason Purpose is a Rule is that as workers today, we are facing more than Alvin Toffler's *Future Shock*; we're now facing option shock. Without highly structured "jobs" and with technology changing our game by the nanosecond, **FutureWork** is oozing with endless potential.

Taking guidance from our elders and/or suggestions from our mentors about how to live our personal and/or professional lives is increasingly more difficult. Their history need not be our destiny. Tomorrow's a clean slate. We have ourselves a window of opportunity if we just get off dead center. Those clichés aside we, more so than any workers in the last century, are now free to carve out a future we can be genuinely wild about.

FutureWork:

Five Rules for a New Game

RULE 1 - PURPOSE

RULE 2 - CONFIDENCE 

RULE 3 - RESPONSIBILITY

RULE 4 - RELATIONSHIP

RULE 5 - FUN

Without me,
there could be no
everybody.

Ashleigh Brilliant

RULE 2

BE CONVINCED YOU HAVE WHAT IT TAKES

CONFIDENCE

Confidence is knowing at the gut level
we have the capability to thrive
in whatever undertaking
we choose.

WHAT WOULD YOU BE DOING IF...?

Picture this scenario:

You're 120 years old sitting in a rocking chair in the Old Employees' Home; you're gumming a bagel; and you're remembering and pondering. Would you be most upset over projects you tried that didn't work or projects you would have liked to try but feel you're too old to do? Sure, research and common sense lead us to the latter.

What would we be doing today and how would we feel about the challenges of **FutureWork** if we had the ultimate confidence in ourselves and couldn't fathom the concept that we might fail? What would we be doing differently in our personal and/or professional lives? What projects and ideas might we implement? What's not being done because we lack the confidence to give it a shot?

Last summer I was in my garage where the workout room is located. I had the door open a few feet to let in some air, and it also let in our little five-year-old neighbor David from across the street. I was riding my stationary bike, and David had never seen a stationary bike before. He had just learned to ride his two-wheeler and had recently removed the training wheels. He had the scrapes on his face for proof. He watched for a couple of minutes and said, "Tom, (he's a modern kid) what's that?" I told him, "It's a bike, Dave, but not like yours. I don't fall off of this one, don't have to ride out in the hot sun, and don't get splashed after a rain. It's neat, isn't it?" He said, "Yeah, but you're not going anywhere!" (Out of the mouths of babes!) "Sure, Dave, but I'm safe."

Do we have enough confidence in ourselves not to have to be "safe?" Because safe is not where we're headed. The training wheels have been removed from our two-wheelers, and we're about to experience the excitement of a whole new ride.

CONFIDENCE: What is it and why is it a Rule?

Confidence is knowing at the gut level we have the capability to thrive in whatever undertaking we choose.

We create our purpose, form our vision, and analyze our reality. If there's a difference between our vision and our reality, that's called a "challenge." We'll experience a pressure to meet that challenge, to close the gap between vision and reality. To close that gap, we must do something different than we are doing today.

To attempt something different, we must have confidence in our ability to succeed. Without confidence, we'll not try as hard. (What's the point in trying; we can't do it anyway.) But with confidence in ourselves, in our ability to do what we want and need to do, we position ourselves for success. We position ourselves for victory over uncertainty. We position ourselves for the excitement of the ride.

REFLECTIONS ON CONFIDENCE

Zapp! You're confident

Nobody gives us confidence. We can't go out and get two pounds of confidence. Confidence is generated and nourished internally, not imposed on us externally. If we don't believe we possess or can get the skills necessary to succeed in **Futurework**, and we choose to work there, we're putting ourselves in a difficult position.

If we don't believe we can do "it," and "it" needs to be done, we will either blunder ahead doing something we don't believe we can do, or we will back off from doing what needs to be done. Either way, we lose.

In our adventurous return to the metaphorical "farm," our confidence will be put to the test. If the jobs we once knew and were good at are still around in the 21st century, it's a good bet doing what we did on those jobs of yesterday will not guarantee tomorrow's success.

A story to illustrate this point appeared in the February, 1995 issue of Training magazine where Alan Downs told the tale of a top-producing retail store manager who had that "second sense" about marketing. His intuition always placed his store among the tops in sales in his organization. Good today skills!

Enter technology - the scanner now used in stores provides management more product movement information than was ever possible with a pencil and paper. Alas, reading and analyzing printouts was not our manager friend's strength. It was not why he was hired; it was not why he had been successful, but it was why he was demoted. Other managers with report-analysis skills passed him by like he was standing still.

Was the manager a bad person? Certainly not! Did he do a bad thing? Only if he wanted to remain a top producer in his industry. Because not keeping up with the trends and the new skills required tomorrow in his industry did him in.

Raising the bar

Experience has taught us we have the capability to perform at whatever level we are currently performing. That gives us confidence up to that level. What happens when the bar is raised as it most certainly will be?

Do we feel at the gut level that we have what it takes to master the new employee/employer relationship, the new loyalty, new independence, new technology — to thrive in the new reality? Can we envision success in an exciting, challenging new game?

The predicament of choosing to go to work each day behaving as if we believe what we're doing will work and not having confidence in our ability to succeed puts our internal and external self in conflict.

When we lie to ourselves, we are a quart low in harmony and integrity, and are overflowing with stress and pressure.

What if, when being brutally honest with ourselves, we have to admit our work life's not working for us? What if we're not excited about **FutureWork**, and we lack the confidence to perform new skills?

Imagine the futility of a life when we're not happy or confident in the game we're playing yet choose to continue playing.

To save everyone a lot of time and aggravation, we must restructure our current jobs to match our confidence or be prepared to go elsewhere where we can use the skills in which we do have confidence.

> **Imagine the futility of a life when we're not happy or confident in the game we're playing yet choose to continue playing.**

Hi! Ho! Hi! Ho! It's off to jail we go

In an illuminating study of 1200 workers, 11 percent of the management and 24 percent of the non management workers said going to work each day was like "going to prison." That's 420 people in that study alone who every day voluntarily go to prison! Why?

Why would people go to jobs every day that they describe as prison? Might they lack the confidence to change and go after a game that really excites them?

I believe we are treated by others the way we have taught others to treat us. I also believe that we are treated by our organizations the way we have taught our organizations to treat us. How are we teaching our organizations to treat us?

Do we teach our bosses we are confident and independent, or do we teach them through our actions we are dependent and scared to death?

> **We are treated by our organizations the way we have taught our organizations to treat us.**

How do we act when our organizations fiddle with our security by even the most subtle means of threatening our salary classification, level, or even, God forbid, our job itself?

Because if management can get somebody to quickly react to fear motivation, they'd be foolish not to use it.

In **FutureWork**, for our good and the good of our organizations, we either have to go out and win the lottery or have the personal confidence to take care of ourselves. If we don't have the confidence to take care of ourselves, who do we think is going to take care of us?

> **If it's not the company's objective to keep us employed, whose objective is it?**

If it's not the company's objective to keep us employed, whose objective is it?

Remember the old proverb warning us, "You should not bite the hand that feeds you." But maybe we should bite it if that hand feeding us interferes with our having the confidence to feed ourselves.

COMPONENTS OF CONFIDENCE

The Circle

Nurturing confidence is simple, but it's not easy. Confidence has many facets which must all fall into place. What part do our beliefs about failure play in generating or increasing confidence? How about risk taking? What's the difference between confidence and self-esteem?

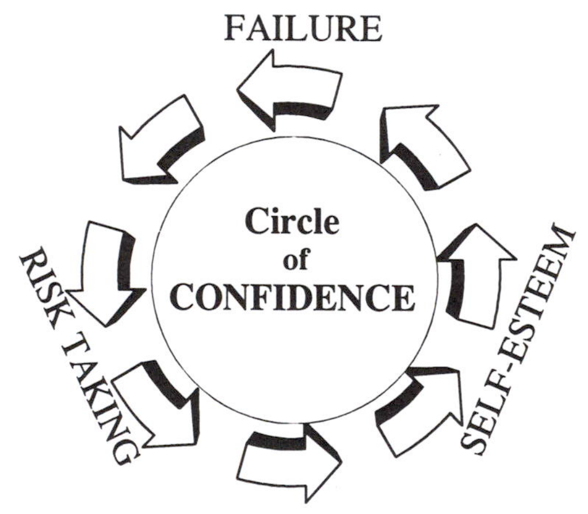

When we overcome the fear of failure, we are free to take a risk. Risks open us to new skills furnishing us with true confidence which lends credibility to our positive self-esteem. Reinforced self-esteem allows us to overcome even greater fear of failure.

All of life's a circle.

Let's examine the major elements of the circle of confidence.

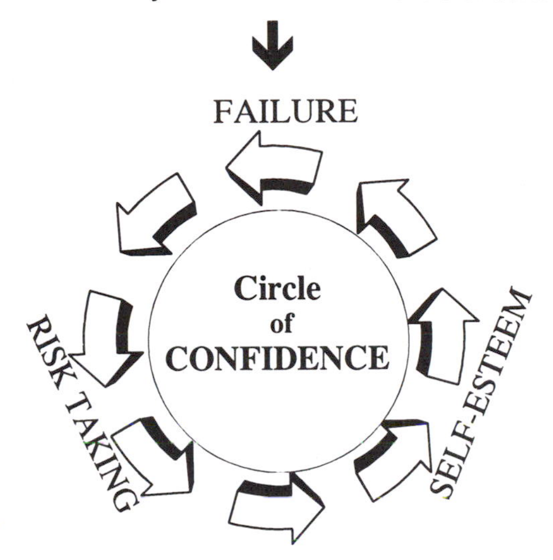

Failure

The entry point of the circle can be anywhere, but for our purposes, let's enter at overcoming fear of failure. If we're not willing to fail, we won't try anything new. We are restricting our confidence to today's level which in all likelihood will not be sufficient for the challenges of **FutureWork**.

Yeah! Failure

To be willing to go counter to our built-in bias against "failure," we must look at failing from another viewpoint. Regardless of what Mrs. Conway said in third grade, failure has benefits. If we don't embrace these benefits, building confidence will be next to impossible. Let's look at three benefits of failure.

The first benefit of failure is that failure is:

- A learning experience.

Everything we do has an outcome. New learning and forming new confidence will occur only when we try something which has an outcome less than we expected. ("An outcome that was less than we expected" is my favorite definition of failure.)

So we have an outcome less than we expected. We should ask ourselves the question, "What did I learn from this?" Don't ask, "Why did I fail?" You might come up with the answer, "I failed because I have the brains of a number two pencil."

"Why did I fail?" conjures up negatives and erodes confidence, whereas "What did I learn?" becomes a learning experience and enhances confidence.

Personal growth and increased confidence take place when we are experimenting with our lives.

Good judgement is said to come from experience, and experience comes from bad judgement. When we succeed, we are often so full of ourselves we don't take time to analyze and to learn from our experiences.

Personal growth and increased confidence take place when we are experimenting with our lives.

The second benefit of failure is that failure is:

- A step to success.

We're going to fail more often than we succeed. How often do we do something to 100% perfection the first time we try (or even the last time)? To succeed more often, we must increase our failure rate, fail our way to success. Art Mortell, in his book, *The Courage to Fail,* says, "Success requires failing most of the time."

I've heard failure described as the "path of least persistence." How often do people lose confidence and quit just before they would have succeeded. Many stop one idea short of success. For example, my uncle was a chemist working for a pharmaceutical company, and he quit at Preparation G. You never heard of Uncle Mike because he lacked the persistence confidence fosters. We must embrace failure, keep trying, and believe no matter what happens, we're still OK.

The third benefit of failure is:

- Development of a sense of humor.

Remember those failures we had at 16 years of age which we didn't want anybody to know. Now they are a major topic of conversation over a tall, cool one. Failure is time sensitive.

If we know we're going to laugh at our failure sometime, why wait? Laugh now.

Failure, if not looked at as a learning experience, a step to success and development of our sense of humor, may lead us to believe we aren't as competent as we thought we were. This lack of confidence will frustrate our ability to flourish in **FutureWork**.

Failure and the organization

Since individuals are what make up an organization, individuals unwilling to accept the benefits of failure have a negative affect on organizational productivity. Let's look at an example.

About a year ago, I was working with a large organization which had decided to reduce the size of its managerial force by 25 percent. That was 2500 managers. If you were the CEO of a company, you would want to keep the best 75 percent of your management work force. If you had already utilized the early retirement offers and you couldn't just fire the old people (there's some kind of law against that), what criteria would you use?

No surprise, he used the performance appraisal. Within a month, 25 percent of the low end of the performance appraisals were gone. And they didn't take their work with them. The company was left with 100 percent of the work and only 75 percent of the people to do the work needing to be done.

> **Just when the company needs creative, innovative, risk-taking, confident people, it's getting a whole immobile employee body more worried about having a job than about doing the job they have!**

The CEO then appeared on closed-circuit TV to speak to the current survivors. He welcomed them to the new lean and mean company and reminded them, in essence, there was 100 percent of the work to do and 75 percent of the people left to do it. He said to be successful, his remaining employees must demonstrate the confidence to be creative, innovative risk-takers and, incidentally, the company was not through downsizing yet!

Do you notice any potential problems? Just when the company needs creative, innovative, risk-taking, confident people, it's getting a whole immobile employee body more worried about having a job than about doing the job they have!

With a fear of failure, risks are not attempted, therefore new skills are not acquired, confidence does not grow and everybody loses.

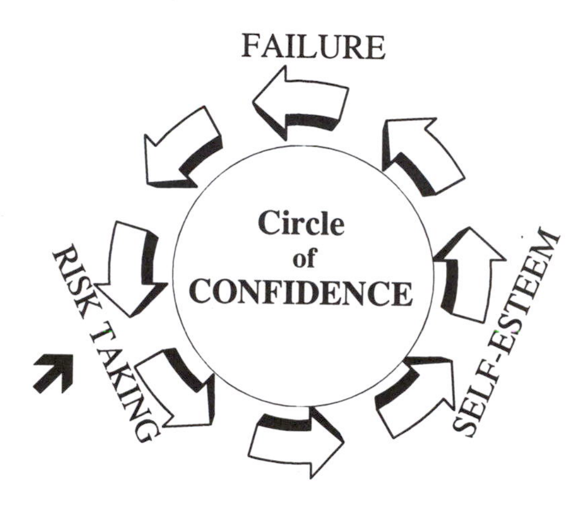

Risk Taking

Having said how we need to push through our current failure comfort zone and take a risk to acquire new skills to gain confidence in new areas, I'll now let you in on a secret — risk taking is easy. It's easy because people don't really take risks, at least not in the context we tend to think about taking risks.

Risk taking, like beauty, is in the eye of the beholder. I believe people will act in a way others may call a "risk" when they have ceased being comfortable where they're at. It's more preferable for them to move to the next level than to remain with the status quo. Here's what I mean:

Biting the Big Apple

Do you feel people who hang glide are taking a risk? Or do you think that for them to exit this life and know they didn't try hang gliding would be perceived by them to be taking a greater risk?

Picture someone who left the security (albeit imagined) of a prestigious job in downtown Manhattan to fulfill his vision and become a potter in Taos, New Mexico. For him, would the risk have been the life change or staying put and taking a daily bite of the Big Apple?

When the here and now gets intolerable for us, we will then take the next step. That next step may be thought of by others as a "risk," but how do we, the "risk takers," view it?

When we discuss risks as a component of the Confidence Rule, take risk to mean what's required from each of us internally to move to that next step.

We don't have to take a risk that's life threatening. Maybe the risk for us, if we have been "stranger challenged" all our life, is to go to a meeting of people we don't know with the objective of networking. Taking a risk is merely taking that next step.

Only if we accept the benefits of failure will we be inclined to take a risk and to move to the next level. Taking a risk means taking a chance, and taking a chance carries a potential to fail.

A way never to lose when playing tennis—never play tennis! If we don't have the confidence to risk anything, we can keep our losses down to zero. But we have also sharply reduced our learning, stifled our confidence, and retreated from success. To top it off, we're not having nearly as much fun as we could have.

If we're not willing to take a risk, we're basically saying we're going to do everything in our power to make it safely to death.

If we're not willing to take a risk, we're basically saying we're going to do everything in our power to make it safely to death.

The risks we are willing to assume are in direct relationship to the consequence we tie to failure. For example:

Same beam, same somersault

If you were an amateur gymnast and had just perfected a somersault on the balance beam, you might feel confident you can do your somersault in the next park district gymnastic tournament and walk away with the blue ribbon. There is a certain risk, but the blue ribbon for your trophy case and your name in the sports section of the paper make the risk worthwhile. If you were to fail and unceremoniously slide off the beam four feet to a padded floor, only the usual audience of about six people and the janitor would know.

But the park district board, to celebrate the 10th anniversary of your community, decides to get some publicity and has the gymnastic event promoted all over the local media. This blitz in the past has been highly successful, and now more than 200 spectators are expected. To give the people something to remember, they are going to suspend your balance beam 50 feet in the air over the tennis court.

> **The risks we are willing to assume are in direct relationship to the consequence we tie to failure.**

Now how confident are you feeling about that somersault of yours?

Same beam, same somersault! If you're successful, you'll still get your ribbon and name in the newspaper. On the other hand, if you're unsuccessful and fail, hundreds of people will witness you becoming intimate with the tennis court. No blue ribbon would be given, and while your name might appear in the paper, it could well be in the obituary column rather than the sports section.

Now in your mind, the consequence of failure outweighs the consequence of success. The agony of defeat outweighs the thrill of victory so the risk may not seem worth it.

When we concentrate on the failure which applying new skills could generate, going to the next level and taking the required risk seem less desirable. Our learning is reduced, creating a loss for both ourselves and our organization.

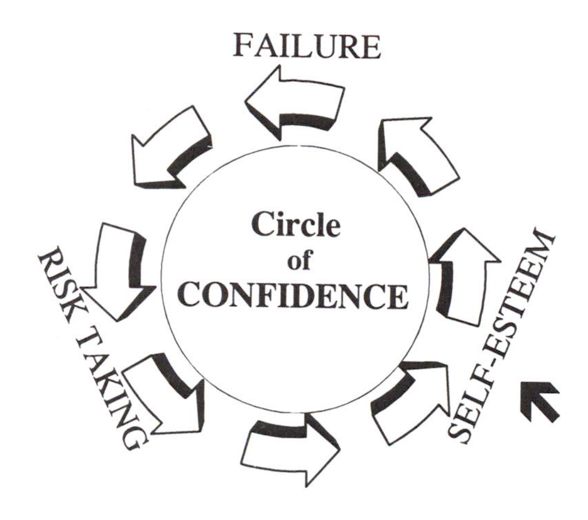

Self-Esteem

Confronting our fear of failure, taking the risk, and learning new skills all add credibility to our confidence level. How does self-esteem fit in the picture?

The chicken or the egg

Does confidence breed self-esteem or does self-esteem breed confidence? Are they really the same article with different names? If so, do we need both?

The dictionary definition loops us around to where we came in, so I researched the difference through official channels. According to the National Council for Self-Esteem (NCSE), self-esteem is "the experience of feeling that you're worthy of happiness and capable of managing life's challenges." I'd have been comfortable with that definition, but in a February 17, 1992 Newsweek article, the National Council's executive director stated he pooled 100 teachers and came up with "27 distinctly different answers" for the definition of self-esteem.

Still a bit confused, I decided to flank the academic answer. After all, that's just what somebody else thinks the word means. Why not ask the people who are in need of this Rule, those folks who are in transitions from here to there. I asked, "Is there a difference between confidence and self-esteem? If there is, does the difference make any difference?"

General consensus was:

We can have confidence without having self-esteem, i.e seeing ourselves able to do what needs to be done while at the same time not feeling pride in ourselves. We can also have self-esteem dripping out of our ears, but not have the confidence we can do anything anybody would want done. So I guess they do have different meanings.

We can survive in **FutureWork** with confidence and no self-esteem, but with self-esteem and no confidence we come up short. But either one without the other is a life that should be lived with a warning label. Confidence without self-esteem is joyless, and self-esteem without confidence is impotent. Both conditions have us acting in opposition to what we believe — a stressful position.

"When I looked in the mirror, I saw an ugly kid who had a hard time reading. I felt terribly isolated and depressed, and was convinced that nobody could or would want to understand me...My natural parents didn't want me; my adoptive parents don't love me. I'm retarded, I'm ugly." Those were words used by an Olympic gold metal winner, Greg Louganis, in his book, *Breaking the Surface*, describing himself at 12 years old.

We see a case of low self-esteem mixed with the confidence to test himself against the world's best in front of millions of people all over the world. Greg is one of the finest divers ever and must be brimming with confidence, but without self-esteem, his life seemed to leave something to be desired.

The best possible world is self-esteem with the confidence to back it up. Let's go with the best.

The Rule for a New Game is Confidence, but to maximize its effectiveness and to keep us away from a series of Maalox moments, let's consider the possession of self-esteem as critical to optimize confidence.

Tough questions

Is there anything in your life you'd give your life for?

It would have to be important, wouldn't it? Richard Bach in his book, *One*, makes the statement, "I gave my life to become the person I am right now." Then he asks the question, "Was it worth it?" Our personal answer to "Was it worth it?" portrays the pride we have in ourselves, our self-esteem.

Bach's question is very powerful, so let me suggest a question I have personally found that gets to the core of his question on how we feel about the worth of our life. My question is, "Am I doing my best?"

If we were to call "time out" periodically and ask, "Am I doing my best in all elements of life? (emotional, intellectual, family, social, spiritual, physical and financial)," our answer will be either positive, negative or neutral. We would know whether we were giving our best shot (positive), not maximizing our potential (negative) or we didn't care (neutral).

Am I doing my best?

When the answer to the question "Am I doing my best?" is either neutral or negative, it begins to chip away at our self-esteem. Anytime we allow ourselves to put forth less than our best effort, we know it, and that to some degree diminishes us in our own minds.

Doing our best does not have to mean being a hero giving the Heimlich maneuver on the evening news. Doing our best simply means taking ourselves to our own personal best, i.e. taking a risk in areas of our lives we feel are important. (This may or may not be work!) To insure "best" thinking doesn't create a race of ulcer-bearing perfectionists, the question, "Am I doing my best?" must be followed by two additional questions: "Do I care?" and "Why do I or don't I care?"

Understanding that doing our best does not mean we must be going 100 percent knock-down drag-out on all cylinders all the time is important. Some time we may choose not to. When you ask yourself if you are doing your best on the social side of life, and your answer is "No," do you care? If you don't care, why not? Perhaps socializing is number six on your life priority list, and there are only 24 hours in a day. If you wanted to do a better job on your social life, you could. You just don't care to and that's fine.

You may or may not choose to devote more time and energy to the financial (work) aspects of life, and others may feel you are wasting potential. But the answer to "Am I doing my best?" like our self-esteem itself, does not and cannot rest with others. The question is personal. The question is: "Am I doing my best in areas of my life I feel are important?" not "Am I meeting others' expectations of me?"

Confidence in ourselves can't be tied to someone or something else.

Confidence in ourselves can't be tied to someone or something else.

"I must be good. Look at all the money, responsibility and the great reserved parking spot my company has deigned to give me." When that stuff goes, and it will, are you then less good? A feeling of confidence and the self-esteem confidence produces cannot be left in the hands of circumstances you don't control.

Self-esteem is not about winning or losing in the eyes of others. Self-esteem is about taking ourselves to our own personal limits in the areas of our lives we have deemed important. If our answer to "Am I doing my best?" in these important areas of life is "Yes," positive self-esteem is significantly enhanced.

Revisiting the circle

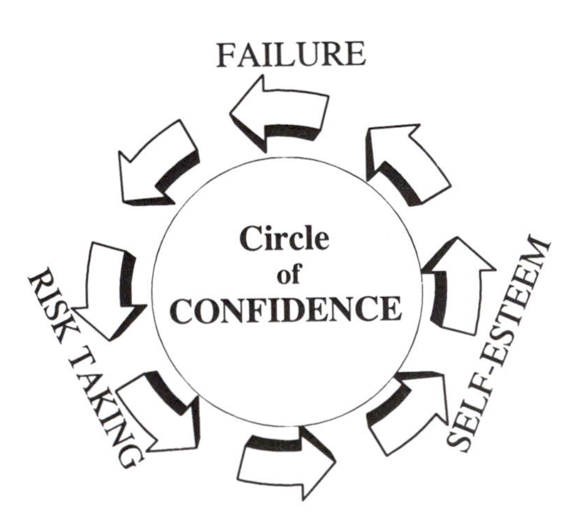

We create our purpose, form our vision and analyze our reality. To close the potential gap between vision and reality, we must possess confidence in our ability to succeed. But confidence can be complicated. When we overcome the fear of failure, we are free to take a risk. Risk taking opens us to new skills furnishing us with legitimate confidence which lends credibility to our positive self-esteem. Positive self-esteem allows us to overcome even greater fear of failure.

All of life's a circle.

OTHERS' VIEWS ON CONFIDENCE

People don't seem to talk much about confidence. If we tell others how good we are, we're seen as egotistical or self-absorbed. (Joe Namath, Muhammad Ali and Mark Spitz are excepted.) Confidence manifests itself more between the lines. Some examples:

☒ Tom Peters, quoted in the Chicago Tribune, said: "Life is pretty simple: You do some stuff. Most fails. Some works. You do more of what works. If it works big, others quickly copy it. Then you do something else. The trick is in the doing something else." We need confidence to do something else, especially when what we've done in the past "worked big."

☒ Robert Fulghum tells an engaging story of confidence in his first book, *All I Really Need to Know I Learned in Kindergarten*. His story is about Larry Walters, a 33-year-old truck driver. Larry always wanted to fly, and he did, but not in the conventional method. He hooked up 45 helium-filled surplus weather balloons to his aluminum lawn chair. He took along a CB radio, some peanut butter and jelly sandwiches, a six-pack of beer and a BB gun to pop some of the balloons when he was ready to come down. This unorthodox contraption worked better than I'm sure even Larry expected. He shot up to over 1100 feet. When the press asked him why he did it, he said: "You can't just sit there."

Fulghum goes on to say. "The human race sits in its chair. On the one hand is the message that says there's nothing left to do. And the Larry Walterses of the world are busy tying balloons to their chairs, directed by dreams and imagination to do their thing." Sure reality says that people can't really fly like birds but again to quote Fulghum, "Somewhere in some little garage, some maniac with a gleam in his eye is scarfing vitamins and mineral supplements, and practicing flapping his arms faster and faster."

Confidence gets us out of our chairs and flapping our arms.

☒ Actor Tony Danza, after a brush with death from a skiing accident, adopted a motto, "If it doesn't really scare me, I don't want to do it."

☒ During a break at one of my sessions, I was speaking to a man who told me a story that could legitimately be described as sad. He was about 65 years old. He and his older sister were the only ones left in the family. Getting together was infrequent. The last time they got to talking about why they didn't keep in better touch. They both came to the realization that the reason why they didn't write to each other was because both lacked confidence in their spelling and punctuation! When they're 120 years old, what will be more important, their relationship or winning the inter-family spelling bee?

☒ Confidence also manifests itself in actions. We don't need a list of strangers to demonstrate confidence. I'm betting you know plenty of people who have sucked it up and gone for the gusto. You can fill in the names:

___________left a good paying job with all of the accustomed benefits and started his/her own business to live out his/her purpose.

___________remained in his/her organization for the same reason.

___________has tested, probed, and questioned the boundaries within his/her organization.

___________lets his/her opinions be known even if they're not the most popular.

__________searches out projects he/she hasn't done before to test his/her limits.

__________passed up a promotion, more money, prestige, and the envy of others in order to do what turns him/her on.

Add these names to the name of the first guy who showed up for work at IBM with a sport coat, and you have some choice examples of confidence.

REALITY OF CONFIDENCE

I think I can; I think I can

The confidence we need to succeed in the 21st century can't be based on wishful thinking. It must be rooted in reality. This is not like the classic story of the 90-year-old man whose answer to his concerned friends as he left for his honeymoon with his 25-year-old bride was, "If she dies, she dies." Our confidence must be reality based.

Psychologist Harold Stevenson from the University of Michigan stated, "American school children rank far ahead of students in Japan, Taiwan and China in self-confidence about their abilities in math. Unfortunately this achievement was marred by the fact that Americans were far behind in actual performance in math."

True confidence must follow not precede actual performance. (As Arnold Glasow noted, "The trouble with ignorance is that it picks up confidence as it goes along.") If confidence in our ability to accomplish a skill is not backed up with our ability to actually accomplish the skill, what good is it?

When we're considering trying something for the first time, and saying we have confidence we can do it, how do we know? We've never done it before! We're using language that's not consistent with reality. What we do have is confidence in a subset of previously accomplished skills. If these past skills all come together in the way we hope they will, we'll accomplish what we're attempting to accomplish.

For example, we might say, "I've stood up before; I've spoken before; I've been in a room full of people before; therefore I am confident I can stand up and speak in front of a room full of people." That logic only goes so far. Reality is satisfied only when you have successfully spoken in front of a room full of people. Only then can you have true confidence in that skill.

> True confidence must follow not precede actual performance.

We may believe that we have the confidence to function in a **FutureWork** state of mind as independent workers, but if we have never clearly defined our purpose, designed our vision, developed and implemented our plan to make that vision come true, we have confidence as far as it goes. For true confidence to function as independent workers, reality says we must function as independent workers.

True confidence follows success. The only place where confidence comes before success is in the dictionary.

Flip side of reality

While focusing on real demonstrated strengths does wonders for one's confidence, reality tells us there is another side. Even as much talent as Microsoft's Bill Gates has, I wouldn't let him take out my appendix. For true confidence, we can't forget our limitations.

Knowing our limitations is tricky business because we're constantly hearing stories like a 98 pound, 98-year-old woman picking up a double trailer truck to rescue a miniature poodle.

If we are 98/98, should we have confidence that we too can pick up trucks? Maybe we can, but as Damon Runyon put it, "The race may not be to the swift nor the victory to the strong, but that's the way to bet." I'd bet on a tow truck.

We must be realistic about our limitations. Having said that, what's real? Here is a caution on establishing limitations.

Part of my weight training routine consists of three sets of ten repetitions (reps) of a certain weight, then three sets of four reps with a much heavier weight. The reason I don't do ten reps with the heavier weight is because I can't; I can only do four. I'm limited.

One day while my mind was listening to an audio-cassette tape and therefore temporarily separated from by body, my body didn't notice the absence because it was busy doing ten reps. At about eight reps, my body began calling my mind's attention to the fact that this set of exercises was getting more strenuous than it should be and maybe we should regroup. So I brought mind and body back to the same place and realized I was beginning rep number nine with the heavier weight! How could that be?

While research tells us that we are most productive when our minds and bodies are in the same place at the same time, I'm not really sure that's always the case. The mind can screw us up if it's not programmed with reality. Reality is I can do ten reps with the heavier weight. I just didn't think I could.

We must be realistic about our limitations in order to effectively eliminate them, but we must also be sure that our perceived limitations are indeed limitations.

SO WHERE DO WE GO FOR CONFIDENCE

Did you ever hear a word you never heard before or notice a fashion statement you never noticed before? Then in the next week everybody you see is dressed in the "new" fashion and using the "new" word. My guess is the word and the fashion have been around; you just weren't conscious of them.

When we become aware of something, we will observe it everywhere we go. We must become aware of our abilities; we need to observe them everywhere we go.

We must have confidence we can succeed in whatever is put in front of us. If we believe it, all of our personal power is in place to make success happen.

If we don't possess the confidence we need, we can get more by formal education, tapes and books. We can use those who have the skill we desire as a role model, or we can take a chance and learn from our experience. But beyond these apparent ways, I believe we possess more skills and abilities which we can convert into confidence than we give ourselves credit for. So let's work with what we already have.

Here are a couple of ideas of how to bring the abilities we currently possess out into the open.

Draw some lines

➭Draw two lines down a sheet of paper. You now have three columns. In column one, write all of your work assignments for the last five years. In the second column, record what you accomplished in each of those assignments. In column three, list what skills and abilities you must have possessed in order to gain those accomplishments. Tear off column three and carry it close to your heart and become aware of all the times each day you use those skills and abilities.

☞Draw two lines down another sheet of paper. Label column one "I can do this," and list all the skills and abilities which will aid you in accomplishing your purpose and in which you have a high degree of confidence. Label column two "I can't do this," and list those skills and abilities for attaining your purpose in which you lack confidence (perceived limitations). Column three, label Action Plan. This is what you're going to do to eliminate or reduce the negative effect on purpose attainment of the items in column two.

Concentrate on the appearances in your life of the items in column one. And since the reality is we can no longer expect the company, or anything outside of us, to provide all the skills we need, we must personally get off dead center and do what we said we were going to do in column three.

☞To implement our action plan and add to our portfolio of skills and abilities, we may feel it takes a lot of something we don't have much of — time. But how big a deal is time? Suppose you could carve out a half hour per day and work on an action plan item. In two years, you would have devoted over 45 eight-hour days to eliminating limitations. How many skills and abilities could you perfect if you devoted 45 days to them?

Ask some questions

☞When you're sitting around with your friends talking about how much you enjoyed this book (that's confidence, eh?), here's an idea to intensify the conversation. Ask your friends to explain the difference between a selection of these words: self-esteem, self-confidence, self-awareness, self-image, self-identity, self-importance, self-knowledge, self-love, self-realization, self-respect, self-efficacy, self-satisfaction, self-worth, self-actualization and/or self-assurance. You may leave the gathering with your eyes spinning around in their sockets, but the discussion should be enlightening and give you a good idea on the areas on which you may wish to concentrate.

Another question is, "If I don't have enough confidence to expand my world and try new things, what will I be doing five years from now?"

We determine our purpose, create our vision, admit reality, conclude what skills are needed, analyze the skills we now possess, decide what else we need and resolve to get them. Nothing fosters confidence like well-placed action.

For more thoughts on confidence, in addition to the books already mentioned, consider reading: *Driving Fear Out of the Workplace* by Kathleen D. Ryan and Daniel K. Oestreich (Jossey-Bass), *Talking to Yourself* by Pamela Butler (Harper-Collins), *Learned Optimism* by Martin E. P. Seligman (Pocket Books).

CONFIDENCE: The short version

We create our purpose, form our vision and analyze our reality. If there's a difference between our vision and our reality that's called a "challenge." We'll experience a pressure to meet that challenge, to close the gap between vision and reality. To close that gap we must do something different than we are doing today.

To attempt something different, we must have confidence in our ability to succeed. Without confidence, we'll not try as hard. (What's the point in trying; we can't do it anyway.) But with confidence in ourselves, in our ability to do what we want and need to do, we position ourselves for success. We position ourselves for victory over uncertainty. We position ourselves for the excitement of the ride.

FutureWork:

Five Rules for a New Game

RULE 1 - PURPOSE

RULE 2 - CONFIDENCE

RULE 3 - RESPONSIBILITY 

RULE 4 - RELATIONSHIP

RULE 5 - FUN

We have only one person to blame,
and that is
each other.

Larry Breck
New York Rangers hockey player

RULE 3

LOOK INSIDE FIRST

RESPONSIBILITY

Responsibility is holding ourselves answerable for what we make of our lives.

OH YOU POOR BABY...

Imagine you arrive home about an hour later than usual. You drop your coat on the floor and yourself on the couch. With a concerned look, your spouse/partner/significant other/companion (being politically correct sure is fascinating isn't it?) observes your glazed appearance and says, "We have to talk. These last couple of months you have been especially uncommunicative with me and the kids. You've been argumentative with the neighbors. You do little else but stare at the TV, and half of the time it's not even on! And you're drinking more than you ever have. What's wrong?"

"I'll tell you what's wrong. My boss won't get off my back; customers are constantly complaining; policies keep changing; rumors about reorganizing are running wild; and all my coworkers have bad attitudes. It's a jungle out there; that's why I'm the way I am."

Your s/p/so/c responds, "Oh, you poor baby, have a glass of wine and relax."

"Thank you," you sigh.

Now let's change the scene a bit. You go home at night about an hour later than usual. And drop your coat on the floor and yourself on the couch. Your s/p/so/c comes over to you and says, "We have to talk. These last couple of months you have been especially uncommunicative with me and the kids. You've been argumentative with the neighbors. You do little else but stare at the TV, and half of the time it's not even on! And you're drinking more than you ever have. What's wrong?"

"This time you respond, "I'll tell you what's wrong. My boss won't get off my back; customers are constantly complaining; policies keep changing; rumors about reorganizing are running wild; and all my coworkers have bad attitudes. So I'm *choosing* to be this loser you see slumped over on the couch. Could you get me another drink please?"

Doesn't quite pack the same punch, does it? If you do get another drink, it's a good bet you'll have to get it yourself. Why? Because now you're taking responsibility, the endangered species of Rules.

RESPONSIBILITY: What it is and why is it a Rule?

We have derived our purpose, created our vision, factored in reality, and established confidence in our ability to succeed in **FutureWork**. If at this critical point, we sit back and hold someone or something else responsible for our success, we'll be getting off the train a couple stops short of our station.

In the **FutureWork** state of mind we'll be asked to exhibit new skills or modify existing skills to meet the requirements of our evolving interactions with work. While tackling new or modified skills can be exciting and challenging, we may not succeed right away.

If we believe our lack of success occurred as a result of the action of someone or something outside of us, then someone or something outside of us will have to change for us ever to succeed.

Waiting for someone or something else to change for us to become as successful as we wish to be can be frustrating at best and paralyzing at worst. How much legitimate control do we have over other people? We may influence their actions, but do we control their actions?

We have things to do to succeed in **FutureWork**. We've worked too hard to give up now. The accomplishment of what we have envisioned for our future cannot be left to the whim of someone or something else. This is no time to drop the reins.

Responsibility is holding ourselves answerable for what we make of our lives.

REFLECTIONS ON RESPONSIBILITY

Rotten nights and pukey mornings

When I was in grade school, I had this belief that anybody older than I could beat me up. I didn't know I had this belief until somebody older beat me up. The Franklin twins did it. (Names are changed to protect the innocent — me. After all they're still older!) The twins, while there were obviously two of them, were only about 1/3 my size (and did I mention they were older?).

After being terrorized every lunch hour for months, I had a little talk with myself and came to the conclusion that I could either hold the Franklins responsible for my sleepless nights and queasy stomach or recognize my responsibility in the matter, confront them and be done with it.

The reason I tell this somewhat embarrassing story is to emphasize the power of taking responsibility. The next lunch hour I went out to the playground, wimped out and took my expected harassment. I went home and blamed the Franklins for not only their extra-curricular activities of the day but also for my rotten night and pukey morning.

A minor cause of mental illness is to make one choice (do nothing) and want the consequence of another (them to go away). Taking responsibility or not taking responsibility is a choice. Are we willing to live with the consequences of our choices?

Whatever the Franklins did to me physically was nothing like what I did to myself mentally. I let people whom I didn't even like control the pleasure of all of my waking hours whether I was with them or not. (Remove Franklin twins and insert boss, customer, rumors, etc.)

I was minimally responsible for the Franklins physical activities, but I was 100% responsible for how I reacted to them.

Dooley did it

I saw a nature special on TV the other day showing cheetahs miss their prey nine out of ten times. We would be a bit short of cheetahs if they got embarrassed and began blaming the length of the grass, the humidity, the weather and those giant flies. If after their seventh miss, they went back to their den all tigered out, and their fellow cheetahs laughed at them like a bunch of hyenas, then they'd spend the rest of their day lion around, taking cat naps, looking like the missing lynx and feline incompetent. (Sorry, got carried away.)

The beauty of being a human animal (other than having prepackaged frozen dinners) is we have imagination. We can use that imagination to gather reasons for our results. These reasons will assist us in learning so we do, or do not, get the same result again. Our imagination can also slam the door shut on learning by providing us someone or something to blame.

If it makes sense to maintain control by accepting responsibility, how come it's not done more often?

Consistent with this topic, I, as a preschooler, blamed my imaginary friend, Dooley. When things went wrong, "Dooley did it." That response seemed to get me out of any consequences my actions might have provoked. When I got too old to use Dooley and too macho to use the Franklin twins, then "My boss did it" fit the bill quite nicely.

Blaming someone or something else, either externally or internally, got me off the hook. Since blaming was rewarded, considering human nature, blaming would be repeated. Therein lies the allure of not taking responsibility.

If we're not responsible for the event, we're therefore not responsible for the result that event created. We're the perfect victims.

This lack of responsibility seems like it would be the answer to a maiden's prayer except that to relinquish responsibility, we must also experience the unfortunate other side of the coin:

No responsibility = no control.

The great giveaway

A major responsibility we give away to others is we allow them to set our limits.

If someone you respected said you were a great motivator of people, would your *people motivation limits* increase? If you were told you're a poor communicator, would your *communication limits* decrease?

Accepting what others have to say about our talents may be described as human nature, but it also puts the responsibility for our communication and motivation skills in the hands of someone who's not us. Of course we value others' opinions, and we should, but how deeply should we value their opinions? How much control over our abilities do we choose to give to others' opinions?

Are others' opinions of us more important to us than our opinions of ourselves?

Are others' opinions of us more important to us than our opinions of ourselves?

Do we determine who we are by looking outside or inside?

Rebels without a clue

Look at the fallacy of the rebellious teen years. Teenagers are not going to let adults dictate to them what they should wear so they all wear clothes in which most adults would not be caught dead. Have the kids really rebelled, or because they're committed to dressing opposite of adults, aren't adults still pulling their strings? Aren't the kids still giving adults the responsibility for what they as kids wear?

If adults started wearing clothes big enough to house the inhabitants of a small nation and pants pulled so low that when they ran they looked like their ankles were sewn together, what do you think those kids would start wearing, maybe three-piece suits? Who's controlling whom?

In tomorrow's world we'll all be experimenting with new skills and modifying old ones. What others have to say regarding our success in doing what needs to be done is input only. We each must take the responsibility as to how we internalize and what we choose to do based on their comments.

As human children, we were dependent for years on others, but some times we carry that dependency too far. Seeing how we came to believe that our responsibility rested elsewhere is not hard. Listen to what goes on around us everyday. Listen to the way we talk, our favorite characters in the movies and on TV. Listen to the lyrics of songs: "I can't live without you," "You make me so very happy," and "You make me feel like a natural woman."

If "you" are so involved with "me," what part do "I" play?

The responsibility scale

There's responsibility and then there's responsibility.

Holding ourselves responsible for what we make of our lives is simple — we're 100% responsible. That's it. If we don't buy that, we're out-of-control victims destined to accomplish our purpose only if "they" allow our purpose to be accomplished.

Holding ourselves responsible for the *events* that occur in our lives is a bit trickier.

To demonstrate what I mean, let's put responsibility for events on a continuum.

Minimum Responsibility 1——————5——————10 Maximum Responsibility

Let's see what the Responsibility Scale looks like in action:

Gwen has been let go from her organization because of poor performance. She set a record for lousy attendance which may never be broken. She was constantly late. When she did show up, she spent half of the time on the job playing games on her PC. As far as responsibility for being let go is concerned, on the Responsibility Scale, Gwen's looking at about a 9.5.

Allan, on the other hand, was let go because his company closed the branch office in which he worked as a star performer. Allan's responsibility for being in the unemployment line hovers around a 2.

Gwen and Allan have decidedly different levels of responsibility for the event of being terminated. But they do share two common situations:

1) They are both currently unemployed.

2) They both have a "10" responsibility for how they react to being unemployed.

Point: We have varying degrees of responsibility for events in our lives, but we have 100% responsibility for what we make of them.

If either Gwen or Allan becomes an alcoholic, loses his or her family and home, and then responds by saying, "The reason I'm sitting here in a grocery cart under an overpass sucking on a bottle of Ripple is because I lost my job," the point has been missed.

A Murphy metaphor moment

Murphy, the dog, liked to take hikes with us in the mountains of central New Mexico. Murphy also liked to jump in mud up to his neck, climb out, and rapidly roll in what ever pile of animal droppings happened to be in the area. In that "earthy" condition, Murphy would come to us, eyes twinkling, begging to be petted. Murphy was an animal unfamiliar with the theories of cause and effect, of an event and consequences.

> **We have varying degrees of responsibility for events in our lives, but we have 100% responsibility for what we make of them.**

What we do creates consequences. We are responsible for our consequences. Not to equate Gwen with Murphy, but if she insists on rolling in it and blames the company for not wanting anything to do with her, she's a woman unclear on the concept.

Notice I gave our friend Allan a "2" on the Responsibility Scale. Why a "2"? The branch was closed; what could he have done? This is a question he must ask himself. This is not a question meant to generate blame, but rather to be more consistent with reality and create options for the future. Could Allan have become the top specialist in an area his company requires? Could he have maintained a closer relationship with the boss? Then even with the branch closing, his services may have been needed or at least endured.

Recognizing his degree of responsibility for the event may not do Allan much good this time, but what about next time? If Allan didn't accept any responsibility, if his condition was solely the results of his company's actions, and he doesn't control the company, Allan will forever be at the mercy of his company, an entity he does not control. Might Allan's time be better spent preparing for the future than being angry about the past?

To be successful in **FutureWork**, we must recognize candidly our level of responsibility for the events that occur in our lives and accept total responsibility for how we react to those events.

Whatever we are not responsible for, we cannot change. Think about the importance of that statement. If we're not responsible, we can't change. If we cannot change, we are not in control. If we are not in control, we're victims. If we're victims, we're unfulfilled, unproductive and unhappy.

> **Whatever we are not responsible for, we cannot change.**

Hard to believe we can build an effective, exciting future staffed with unfulfilled, unproductive, and unhappy victims.

But a future staffed with people taking responsibility for their lives, internalizing what they have learned from experience and moving on toward their goals is a sight to behold.

Taking responsibility gives us back control and voids the victimhood.

COMPONENT OF RESPONSIBILITY

Control

If we relinquish responsibility, we give up control of our lives because we are declaring someone or something else is in charge. How scary is that? — SOMEONE OR SOMETHING ELSE IS IN CHARGE OF OUR LIVES. And we're not only letting it happen; we're making it happen!

When is the last time you blinked

Why is control (by control I mean the ability to make something happen or not happen when we want it to happen or not happen — total control) important for success in the **FutureWork** state of mind?

When we give up control, we are put in a position of stress, not the good kind but the negative kind — the kind of stress where you're so uptight you haven't blinked in a week. That kind of stress results in diminished performance. For example:

What are some attributes needed to be a respected manager, teammate, coworker or good friend to help a fellow employee going through the pressures of today's changing work environment?

Good listening skills, patience and a sense of humor would be some solid answers to that question. But consider how easy it would be to be a patient, good listener with a sense of humor if you just get in the office and your boss is crawling all over your back. Customer complaints are stacked up; policies have changed for the umpteenth time. Rumors of reorganizations are running wild, and the only people complaining more than your customers are your coworkers.

Right at this tense moment a coworker comes to your desk and says, "Do you have a couple of minutes to listen to some problems I have?" You bellow, "You have problems! I have a boss all over me, policies written on an Etch-A-Sketch, etc., etc., etc."

Not that you don't know how to be patient, listen and display a sense of humor, you're just choosing not to because of events that are occurring that are out of your...control.

We're allowing the events to control the implementation of our skills. We don't control the events; therefore we don't control the implementation of our skills. Powerless position to be in!

Taking responsibility for how we respond to uncontrolled events and not blaming the events gives us back the control we need to implement the skills we own.

We must take responsibility to gain personal control.

Control — big deal

Personal control may not seem like a big deal considering the major tests we're being given daily. But what control do we have over our organization, bosses, coworkers? So while personal control may seem to be a small feat to achieve, it's the most practical.

Shad Helmstetter tells us in his book, *Choices*, "If each of us did nothing more than to take responsibility for ourselves, none of us would have to wish that we could change the world."

We're going into a time we haven't experienced, a time most of us would not have imagined or initiated.

We'll need all of our wits about us to accomplish what we want to accomplish. By accepting appropriate responsibility for our actions, events and lives, we are in charge, in command and in control. Getting excited about the control responsibility provides is in our best interest.

All of this pandemonium about change is wrapped around the issue of control. Change can be negative when we don't control it. If change is our idea, looking at change as a positive challenge is easier. My family's move from Chicago to Albuquerque was our idea. That made all of the inconveniences of a cross-country move exciting and challenging. If someone had told us we had to move, every activity would have been viewed, at best, as a giant pain in a body part.

FutureWork mind set will be the same. If we take control by assuming responsibility, creating a future consistent with our purpose, and initiating change on our terms, we can turn a potentially painful journey into a challenging and exciting trip.

If today were a fish

Did you ever have a bad day?

Think back to your last bad day at work. This may not be a long trip down memory lane, but think back to the last day at work where if the day were a fish you'd have thrown it back. What happened to classify the day as bad?

When you thought of the events of the day, were the first causes coming to your mind that the day was miserable because: the boss, policies, and coworkers or did you think, "Yes it was a miserable day, but when all was said and done regardless of what went on, I chose to make myself nuts." If that wasn't basically your answer, don't feel like Clayton Moore.

A recent study illustrated that 77% of the people asked blamed something outside of themselves for their results. More than three out of four people did not take responsibility for their results. I personally think 77% is low.

Think about your reasons for a bad day. Think about any recent conversation with coworkers or family members. When their bad days are discussed, was the word "I" even mentioned? How many people do we know who take responsibility for their present condition?

Pain, pain go away

If you worked for your organization for the next 25 years, how many of these daily events that stretch you to the breaking point would go away? Some day will there be no boss to bother you, only happy customers and stable policies? I think not. So then we're choosing to go to a place every day, today and tomorrow, that is teeming with events we choose to let drive us to the edge.

> **How many people do we know who take responsibility for their present condition?**

During one program I was conducting, a women claimed what got in her way of accomplishing what she wished to accomplish was "unplanned emergencies." We talked at the break, and she told me she was a nurse at a hospital. Would you care to guess in what department she worked? The emergency room! Was she waiting for people to make a reservation? A government worker was being driven batty by the bureaucracy, a customer service person by irate customers! As if these events were a surprise!

Most of the events which create negative stress in our work life are inherent in that life. If we choose to place responsibility for our lack of success on these events which are native to the world of work and over which we have no control, we are in effect choosing to be less fulfilled and less productive than we have the potential to be.

If these undesirable events and other events over which we have little or no control are indeed responsible for our less than desirable results, I would suggest that tomorrow before going into work, call and ask whomever answers, "Is the boss going to be all over me today? Are there going to be anymore rumors? Will there be irate customers?" If the answer is "yes" to any question, pull the sheets up over your head and go back to sleep because you're going to have a rotten day and the company will be paying you for less than your best work.

The reason so many folks tend to blame events outside of themselves for their lot in life is that if someone or something else is not responsible, then there is only one other choice.

I would like to strongly recommend we make that other choice.

We are responsible to some degree for the events that occur in our lives and 100% responsible for how we react to those events. Accepting our responsibility sets us up for success in **FutureWork.**

The reason so many folks tend to blame events outside of themselves for their lot in life is that if someone or something else is not responsible, then there is only one other choice.

Adam and Eve

Eluding responsibility is nothing new. Adam blamed Eve, and Eve blamed the snake (and the snake didn't have a leg to stand on). The only two people on earth, and they found somebody or something else to blame. How much easier it must be for us!

Consider the people suing the liquor and tobacco companies for making the people use their products. Also how about:

◆The family of a man killed on his way home from work at Coors brewery who sued the brewery over Coors' policy of allowing beer to be drunk during breaks. I can just picture this guy during a break being held in a hammer lock while his foreman poured beer down his throat. Where was this worker's responsibility for not drinking and driving?

◆The woman in my town of Albuquerque who spilled hot coffee on herself and sued McDonalds for having the coffee too hot. Initially she was awarded $2.6 million (later reversed to a much smaller sum). Not only did the woman have the guts to sue over her own clumsiness, but what was the jury smoking?

◆A young thief in Massachusetts who stole a car from a parking lot and was killed while driving it. The family sued the owners of the parking lot for not having procedures in place to prevent the theft.

The list goes on and on past the point of nausea.

These are all tragic events, but where is the personal responsibility? As Dale Dauten, a columnist for King Features Syndicate, said "If God could be sued, we'd have no mountains." Where does the buck stop?

Murder has become the third ranked cause of on-the-job death. This looming preference for fixing responsibility on someone or something outside of ourselves increases the chance of violence. People no longer see themselves personally responsible in any degree for the events that make up their lives. Something outside of themselves, that they do not control, is threatening their very being and must be destroyed.

A **FutureWork** state of mind is ours to make or break, and that responsibility cannot be avoided.

OTHERS' VIEWS ON RESPONSIBILITY

☒ In his book, *A Nation of Victims*, Charles Sykes quotes a statistic contending if we totaled up all classes who feel they are an oppressed minority, it would equal 374% of the population!

If we continue to labor under the misconception that we are victims of everything and anything going on around us, we are less likely to take personal initiative. As victims, we are less likely to determine what responsibility we have for our current state of affairs and to get on to fixing them.

Then, of course, there are the lawyers. The US has 70% of world's lawyers. This is not a put-down of lawyers, but they couldn't survive if we each accepted our share of responsibility and stopped trying to force others to take on responsibility that is rightfully ours.

☒ A writer, P. J. O'Rourke, stated in a speech: "There is only one basic human right, the right to do as you please unless it causes others harm. With it comes the only basic human duty, the duty to take the consequences." O'Rourke didn't say the duty to find someone or something else to take our consequences.

☒ Nick Nolte's character, a basketball coach in the movie, *Blue Chips*, said "Two reason's I'm incapable of cheating. One, if I break the rules and I get caught, I'll get kicked out of coaching and the second reason, I might not get caught." Recognizing our responsibility and living with it can be tough.

☒ Louis Nizer, an astute lawyer, when asked about the part luck played in his success, said he found luck came to him most often at about 3 a.m. in the law library. I believe luck plays an important part in our lives (how else could we explain the success of those people we don't like?), but the responsibility to be in the law library at 3 a.m. is ours.

☒ Wayne Dyer wrote in *You'll See it When You Believe It,* "You cannot get to a sense of purpose, and live a life of harmony and balance while simultaneously allowing someone else to dictate your thoughts and actions." "...Enlightenment demands that you take responsibility for your life. Responsibility means literally to respond with ability." Dyer is reinforcing the fact we are in charge; we have the ability to respond, to get a jump on things, to not wait for someone or something else to respond. We're in charge; we're in control.

☒ Richard Bach in his book, *One*, says "We are given a block of marble when we begin a lifetime, and the tools to shape it into a sculpture — We can drag it behind us untouched, we can pound it into gravel, we can shape it into glory....How can we resent the life we've created for ourselves. Who's to blame, who's to credit, but us? Who can change it anytime we wish, but us?" Bach doesn't say we should give our coworkers, rumors, policies or our boss the hammer and let them do with us as they please. We would never accept being forced to relinquish our personal power, and yet that's exactly what many of us voluntarily do.

REALITY OF RESPONSIBILITY

If we accept the concept of self-responsibility, the reality is our self-esteem is being set up to be stroked or stomped.

If we are indeed responsible, and our life is turning out according to our vision — good for us, and score one for self-esteem. But if we are responsible and our life is going down the porcelain

If we accept the concept of self-responsibility, the reality is our self-esteem is being set up to be stroked or stomped.

convenience, we could be scooping our self-esteem up with a shovel.

I firmly believe taking responsibility for our lives is worth the risk. Because if we don't take responsibility, then something else must be responsible. Then we have, in essence, given up control which is a far greater impediment to our success in **FutureWork** than knowing we're responsible for a less than desired result.

They just don't care

None of the changes we've gone through or will be going through care what we think of them!

Reorganizations don't care if we think they're exciting or terrifying. They just are, and will continue to be. If we choose to give responsibility for the success of our lives over to the management concept of the moment, that is certainly our choice. But remember we are allowing a concept that could care less to dictate the pleasure and fulfillment of our days.

If it weren't so true, it would sound silly, wouldn't it?

> **The reality is rejecting responsibility comes easily because, if we do accept it, then we have to admit the person we are today is one chosen by us.**

The reality is if we don't take responsibility, we lose control. We lose control in the worst way, to — elements, concepts, people who may not even be aware we exit. Elements, concepts and people have a life of their own.

Also if we're not responsible for our results, how do we establish an accurate sense of self-esteem? How can we have pride in ourselves if everything we are is a result of something outside of us?

(The Rule of Responsibility is not discounting the part religion plays in the outcome of our lives. For the purpose of our discussion, responsibility is what we can do for ourselves here on earth. As the old saying goes, "Pray to God as if he is the only one who can help and act as if he doesn't exist." It's the acting part we're talking about.)

The reality is rejecting responsibility comes easily because, if we do accept it, then we have to admit the person we are today is one chosen by us. Difficult position, but true and very empowering!

We have put all the structures in place to be who we are. If we feel that's too heavy a burden to carry, look at it another way. While we have responsibility and the accountability responsibility entails, we also have control and the power control brings to the game. That's a compromise we should be willing to make any time.

SO WHERE DO WE GO FOR RESPONSIBILITY

We take it. We recognize when we're giving it up, and we take it back.

Right now I'm choosing...

The laws of Nature:

1) The laws always work.
2) Ignorance of the laws doesn't change their effect
3) The laws don't care what we think of them.

A person's ignorance of gravity doesn't mean he will fly when he jumps off a ten-story building. We, as human beings, are responsible for what we make of our events, and just because we don't know it doesn't make it any less true.

So let's get to know our responsibility.

➯The best way to get us thinking in a new way is awareness and repetition. In the one and only drivers' safety education class I attended while employed by a large corporation, the instructor had us drive a car and vocalize what we were seeing while driving. "There is a man stepping off the curb to my right." "The car ahead is signally for a left turn." After about one-half hour of this, I was amazed how aware I became of what was going on around me.

Let's try this same approach, with the exception of the car, for becoming aware of responsibility. The following concept comes from a book by Nathanel Branden, *Honoring the Self*.

The key phrase is:

Right now I'm choosing to ________, and I take responsibility for that.

Examples:

Right now I'm choosing to stay late at the office, and I take responsibility for that.

Right now I'm choosing to make dinner for my family, and I take responsibility for that.

Right now I'm choosing to be a real dork, and I take responsibility for that.

Right now I'm choosing to go to the zoo with my kids, and I take responsibility for that.

Right now I'm choosing to be really unhappy over the changes at work, and I take responsibility for that.

Practice:

Right now I'm choosing to ________, and I take responsibility for *that.*

Poor, poor, pitiful me

↬Another way to create an awareness is to tell a story to someone about when you were a victim and really get into your victimization. Then go back with your listener (or a whole group of people if you really want an eye opener), analyze the story, accept responsibility, and examine where you could have done something to change the result.

This approach appeared in a book, *You Can't Afford the Luxury of a Negative Thought,* by John-Roger and Peter McWilliams.

For more thoughts on responsibility, in addition to the books already mentioned, consider reading: *Seven Habits of Highly Effective People* by Steven Covey (Simon & Schuster), *Reengineering Yourself* by Daniel Araoz and William Sutton (Bob Adams, Inc.), *Empires of the Mind* by Denis Waitley (William Morrow).

RESPONSIBILITY: The short version

If we relinquish responsibility, we give up control of our lives because we are declaring someone or something else is in charge. How scary is that? — SOMEONE OR SOMETHING ELSE IS IN CHARGE OF OUR LIVES. And we're not only letting it happen; we're making it happen!

We're going into a time we haven't experienced, a time most of us would not have imagined or initiated.

We'll need all of our wits about us to accomplish what we want to accomplish. By accepting appropriate responsibility for our actions, events and lives, we are in charge, in command and in control. Getting excited about the control responsibility provides is in our best interest.

FutureWork:
Five Rules for a New Game

RULE 1 - PURPOSE

RULE 2 - CONFIDENCE

RULE 3 - RESPONSIBILITY

RULE 4 - RELATIONSHIP 

RULE 5 - FUN

Our concern is not how to worship in the catacombs, but how to remain human in the skyscrapers.

Abraham Heschel

RULE 4

REMEMBER YOU'RE NOT ALONE

RELATIONSHIP

Relationship is recognizing the part
other people play in our lives
and
valuing the strength
we derive from this connection
with others.

CARL

Carl was a retired pharmaceutical salesman. He wore his hair in a tight crew cut like he did during his days in the Corps. A slight man with glasses and an ever-present bow tie. You get the picture.

No, you probably don't. To really get the picture of Carl, you didn't need to see him, you needed to experience him. I first got "Carled" the day after I met him.

Carl in his retirement took up public speaking. He called his company, *People and Pride*. His purpose was to help people feel good about themselves.

Carl was passionate about his purpose. When he spoke he was no Zig Ziglar, but then neither was Zig a Carl. Carl approached his business differently than many people. For example, his business card was cut from construction paper. The card had a pasted picture of Carl taken at one of those "go in the booth and get four pictures for a dollar" kind of places. He was also different in another significantly more substantial way. Carl really tried to relate to people.

Carl wondered until the day he died why most people never responded when he called them or sent them something in the mail. Carl thought responding to another's gesture was common courtesy. I wonder where he could have come up with a strange idea like that?

Getting back to me getting "Carled" for the first time, I met Carl at a talk I was giving. The following day the newspaper had a write-up about the event, and my name was mentioned. The next day I received by mail the article, laminated on a piece of cardboard, with a note of congratulations from Carl. Such acknowledgement is not an everyday occurrence in my life.

From that day, every time my name was mentioned anywhere in print the next day a note would come on a laminated piece of card-board. If the publicity was not in print, Carl just sent a note.

Carl didn't do what he did for money; he did it because it fit his purpose. He spent hours scouring newspapers, finding stories, laminating them and mailing them off to give the recipients tangible evidence of why they should feel good about themselves.

Carl's endeavors were not about getting a reply. But a reply would have been nice.

I knew Carl about three years before he died. Unless he had a death bed conversion, Carl moved on to the big stage in the sky being confused and a bit hurt over the lack of response to his reaching out. He wouldn't be human if he weren't a bit hurt, but Carl didn't have to be confused. The reason is obvious.

The people Carl thought enough of to spend time, energy, money and a piece of himself on were too busy to respond.

Carl didn't mean business, status or power to others. He was just a little guy with a bow tie and a homemade business card reaching out to touch other human beings.

I wonder where he could have come up with a strange idea like that?

RELATIONSHIP: What it is and why is it a Rule?

We have our purpose translated to a vision matched with reality. We possess the confidence to do what we want to do, and we accept responsibility for our vision's fulfillment. Now let's get to-gether to mutually support each other.

The trip to the mental state of **FutureWork** is going to be an exciting challenge. The time to choose and nourish those with whom we wish to share the ride is now.

As Larry Wilson from the Pecos River Learning Center has been heard to say, "I have to do it myself and I can't do it alone." That's not a Zen koan; it's the essence of the Rule of Relationship.

The term, relationship, is an overall umbrella for many levels of human interaction. Our relationships extend from the nodding acquaintance, to the friend on our party guest list, to the person to whom we tell our most intimate thoughts. Relationships can be found on or off the "job" employed by another or self-employed.

This discussion of Relationship as a Rule for a New Game is about the importance of all relationships to **FutureWork**, regardless of the level or context of the relationship. Relationships as discussed here are about connecting with others for mutual benefit.

Relationship is recognizing the part other people play in our lives and valuing the strength we derive from this connection with others.

REFLECTIONS ON RELATIONSHIP

Rowing merrily down the stream

FutureWork thinking brings us a new playing field. Each of us has as good a chance at success as anyone else if we utilize the Rules to maximize our talents. Since all of us together have more knowledge than each of us alone, to maximize our individual and collective talents, sharing our skills and abilities makes good sense.

To be thrilled about sharing, we must understand Relationship as a Rule for **FutureWork** is not built on the law of scarcity (there's only so much work so I'd better hoard mine), but on the law of abundance (work creates work and there will be plenty for us all).

Our philosophy must be, "If your end of the boat goes down, so does mine." Together we row merrily down the stream.

Statistics abound declaring information is doubling every two to three years or less in almost every field. We can't know it all — we wouldn't want to know it all. What we don't know, somebody else will know. Synergy, the power of the team, the power of maintaining relationships!

Mr. Guilty or Ms. Lonely

In these last few years, organizations have played havoc with relationships by downsizing our coworkers right out of their chairs and restructuring fellow employees into competing business units. Organizations have been making decisions on who to keep and who not to keep by ranking according to competitive performance appraisals.

None of these all-too-common occurrences creates the desire to bond with our teammates.

The situation is more like wartime when soldiers don't want to get too close for fear of losing their fox hole buddy. And if they do wind up losing a buddy, they feel guilty for being survivors. We're either running around being Mr. Guilty or Ms. Lonely. This situation is not good for relationships, personal or organizational.

To unleash the energy of relationships, we must reverse this trend. We must reestablish our connectedness to others for success in **FutureWork.**

Independent relationships

Over the last few years, I have talked and written extensively on the need for independence in the workplace; now I'm talking about building relationships. What gives?

Yes, we need independent relationships. What we need to be independent from is the financial and social umbilical cord tying us to an organization. That's an unacceptable situation. If we are dependent on an organization but that organization is not necessarily dependent on us, the relationship is too one-sided to be healthy.

> **If we are dependent on an organization but that organization is not necessarily dependent on us, the relationship is too one-sided to be healthy.**

We also need to be independent of our organization to be effective team members. The relationship built between members of a team is based on trust. Trust, as we will see later, is based on a consistency among what is said, what is done, and what is believed. That degree of consistency will require, on occasion, team members to exhibit independence and go against the "group think" of the team.

If we are not independent, we are not as valuable to the team.

Maybe lack of independent team members is the reason author Jerry Harvey stated in *Abilene Paradox*, "People in groups tend to agree on courses of action which, as individuals, they know are stupid." If everyone on the team, in order to maintain a false concept of harmony, accepts solutions which each knows are stupid, what good is the team?

Relationships, whether with people as individuals or with those on teams, require independence to maximize their effectiveness. Maximized relationships are valuable to us, to our organization and society in general.

Society in general

Technology is not necessarily bringing us together. Telecommuting to the virtual office, while important for efficiency, good for the bottom line, and environmentally sound, paints a pretty bleak picture from the relationship standpoint.

A survey by Roper Starch Worldwide Inc. shows that Americans are cutting back on the number of friends they see regularly. In 1994 Americans saw four friends in a two-week period, down from 5.4 friends in 1983. What do we think will happen to that number when more of us work out of our homes, FAX to the company library for training videos, attend meetings over two-way teleconferencing, shop and bank via computer, then, after a busy day at the keyboard, settle on our couch with a tub of microwave popcorn summoning up a movie-on-demand on our satellite dish?

In unpredictable times when it seems we most need the comfort and connectedness of human interaction, we're confronted with rapid technological advancement. Given the reality of our world, we must work extra hard at nullifying the dehumanizing aspects of galloping technology.

What can we do to simulate human relations in high-tech times? Let's look at one small but significant everyday example.

Telephoning into the black hole

I hear this complaint all too often — more people than ever are not returning telephone calls. I don't mean within the acceptable standard of twenty-four hours; I mean ever! People perceive themselves as too busy. Something has to go.

They rationalize that what they are eliminating is just another telephone call, but in reality what is being sacrificed is of far greater significance. They are sacrificing common courtesy.

This sacrifice is doing more than hurting relationships with others. Not drawing upon, tapping into, responding to or relating to other human beings also caps organizational productivity.

How so?

In the quest for improved organizational results, we must be careful to remind ourselves of the basic human input to bottom-line attainment. What are the basics of management, teamwork, communications, sales and customer service, all essential for organizational productivity, if not the relationships between us human beings?

Not drawing upon, tapping into, responding to or relating to other human beings is also caps organizational productivity.

Stew Leonard, when talking about how he hires his employees for his retail food store, said, "You can teach them cash register, but you can't teach them nice."

"Nice" is a good start for personal and organizational productivity and a key ingredient in the Rule of Relationship.

Failure to return telephone calls may not be that big a deal by itself, but it may well be a symptom of the disease common in too many people who make up organizations in today's frantic society — "forgetting the basics-itis."

Acknowledging others' attempts at connectedness, while plain, old, common courtesy, is also perhaps a small way to nullify the negative aspects of technology, and it's something we can do, if we choose.

Common courtesy — business style

As a part of the promotion for my first book, *From the Inside Out: How to Create and Survive a Culture of Change*, complimentary copies were sent to the top executives of 300 major companies for mutually beneficial purposes.

While not naive enough to believe that the executives would curl up on a cold winter's night in front of the fireplace with a cognac and my book, we did expect the courtesy of a reply. After all, how long can it take an executive assistant to produce a standard acknowledgement note? Also we were potential or current customers of every one of those companies.

How many of North America's largest companies do you think chose to acknowledge receipt of a gift from another human being, not to mention a current or potential customer?

Fifteen!

Only five percent of American business, companies such as IBM, Chrysler, Merck & Co., Marriott Corporation, GE and US West Communications committed to and demonstrated that level of customer (human) relationship.

(And it's a sure bet the companies which did not reply are busy devoting significant dollars to customer service programs and wondering why implementing improved customer service is so tough.)

Do you think the other 285 companies didn't know how to reply? If their Chairman of the Board sent something — anything — to the CEO — would it be at least acknowledged? I guess we, as potential customers, were not deemed as important as someone on their payroll might be. What do you think our attitude is today toward these companies?

Putting business considerations aside, what we're dealing with here is a demonstrated lack of common courtesy practiced by individuals in the organization in the name of the organization.

What might your organizations be doing or not doing to form relationships with its customers, current or potential? More importantly what might you be doing? Any Carls left unacknowledged?

We build mutually beneficial relationships by communicating with others, trusting them and being open to their ideas, no matter how foreign to us those ideas (or those people) may be. Let's look at three components of the Rule of Relationship. We'll start with communications, and then move on to trust and diversity.

COMPONENTS OF RELATIONSHIP

Communications

As people in organizations immigrate to the state of **FutureWork**, we are often asked for help in developing the new skills those organizations perceive as required. The skill most requested is communications. "Help our people communicate."

Since communications are such a vital element in relationship, we're always pleased when an organization desires to improve them. But just what does improving communications mean?

Why is communication not occurring? Is the telephone system inadequate, FAX not working, or the Internet too confusing? Or maybe the office layout is such that people have difficulty getting to each other? Is the organization so deeply layered that communication gets lost in the maze? Or is it that every time an employee opens his or her mouth Esperanto comes out instead of the intended language? Just what does it mean when organizations say, "Help our people communicate?"

It typically means we aren't telling each other the truth.

If we're harming our relationships through lack of honest communications today, we must be choosing not to communicate honestly.

Out of the mouths of babes

When a seven year old tells you you're ugly, you're ugly.

That old truism tells me that we know how to deliver open and honest communications; we can tell the truth. We did it when we were seven years old. If we're harming our relationships through lack of honest communications today, we must be choosing not to communicate honestly.

Of course, we will not build lasting relationships by deliberately hurting other people, but in an attempt to be loved by everyone or to avoid potential confrontation, we may keep inside ourselves issues best dealt with outside.

In these stormy times, relationships are strained because people are omitting or misrepresenting major pieces of information.

The boss isn't telling the employee what she knows about the future due to misguided policies or a controlling management style. The employee's not telling the boss what's really needed to do the job more effectively because the employee sees that as being "not my job." Or is he or she afraid of the consequences? For example:

Boo

Considering the culture of your organization today, is the relationship between boss and employee such that it would be acceptable for people to be open and honest and tell their bosses if they're scared? I don't mean specific bosses. One-on-one, I'm sure you can find some open relationships, but what about the culture of your industry? Your organization?

Is it in the culture of the organization to communicate those kinds of feelings? Usually we can express feelings when we feel angry. This is an acceptable feeling in today's work environment since it's regarded as macho (or femcho, as the case may be). What about a more vulnerable feeling such as being scared?

Is anyone scared in your organization? Do scared employees generate different behaviors at work than those employees who are challenged and excited? Do scared employees, over the long run, due to their different behaviors, generate different results than the challenged and excited employees? Of course.

So why are work relationships such that we often don't communicate our feelings honestly? What do we think would happen to the boss/employee relationship if we told our bosses we're scared? (Many folks are afraid of being perceived as wimps and seeing this as a negative on their performance review.)

In **FutureWork**, relationships must be able to include honest communications without fearing externally imposed negative consequences, like a pathetic performance review or a punch in the nose. And our confidence must be such that receiving a ration of well-intentioned honesty is OK.

For the good of us all and the strength of our relationships, we must encourage others to confront us, to push against us and to test our conviction at every turn. That's a healthy relationship.

We have the inherent know-how to communicate honestly. Choose to combine that knowledge with a sincere desire to foster, strengthen and enlighten relationships, and we'll equip ourselves and our organizations for the excitement and challenges waiting just around the corner.

Imagine the strength of the relationships and the power, energy and passion that would run loose in an organization whose core value was, "Always communicate the truth."

Imagine the strength of the relationships and the power, energy and passion that would run loose in an organization whose core value was, "Always communicate the truth."

Trust

You can be the most truthful of communicators but that will do nothing for your relationships if the people with whom you're communicating don't trust you any more than they'd trust a $2.95 Bungee cord.

How's trust in your organization?

Will management do what it says it will do? Will team members do what they say they will do?

How strong can a relationship be if the trust level's elevator doesn't go to the top floor? In the future, we will not want to take the time from doing something we feel is important to play somebody else's futile game.

In whom do you place your trust?

The people in whom I place my trust are those people who, on a consistent basis, behave externally the way they believe internally.

If they tell me they'll do something, they mean to do it, and will do everything in their power to get it done. If they don't believe in a certain policy or procedure, they will let me know. They tell and act the truth as they believe it to be. This truthfulness brings them consistency, harmony and personal integrity.

How's trust in your organization?

I don't have to like them, but I do trust them.

Trust, relationship and the organization

Considering relationship is built on trust, feeling the warm fuzzy of mutual benefit in our relationship with our organizations is difficult when it looks as if we're being used as pawns in the bottom-line chess game. In the words of the Little Red Riding Hood fable, we've gone from the protection of granny to "All the better to eat you, my dear."

Organizations will have to go some to rebuild employee/employer relationships. In many organizations, trust is shot. Rebuilding trust will be rough, but doable. Organizations must commit to the truth and display a consistency between what they say and what they do from this moment on.

Organizations must commit to the truth and display a consistency between what they say and what they do from this moment on.

We, as workers, may not like the truth, but if consistency and honesty are shown, trust will develop, and a mutually beneficial relationship will be reestablished.

Does a big bear sprint in the woods?

How long does it take an organization to get the trust necessary to build a mutually beneficial relationship? How long to lose it?

The following story is an example of how fast we can lose trust.

A couple of friends of mine, Mitch and Rick, were hunting in the mountains of northern New Mexico. They heard a noise from behind them. When they looked up, they saw the biggest bear in the woods coming down the hill, headed right for them. Mitch sat down and started changing from his hunting boots to his running shoes. Rick said "Why are you changing shoes; you'll never be able to outrun that bear." Mitch said, "I don't have to outrun the bear; I only have to outrun you!" We can lose trust very quickly. Ask Rick.

Trust often comes slowly and goes quickly. Why? Can't trust come quickly and go slowly? Does a person have to earn trust over an extended period? Can't they start off with it?

We can approach trust either way. Start off with no trust and build up trust over time until the other person has demonstrated trustworthiness. Or we can give them complete trust up front and begin pulling back if they start changing from their hunting boots to their running shoes.

The quicker the trust builds, the quicker the relationship builds.

Truth tests a relationship

Telling the truth as we see it is easy; the consequences may be hard. There's a reason for the saying, "Truth hurts." When we make a statement or perform a behavior perceived by the other party as negative towards them, we're chipping away at the very relationship we're trying to build.

If trust contains honesty and honesty can hurt the relationship trust was supposed to enhance, something is amiss. If being honest hurts a relationship, maybe the relationship is not as strong as it needs to be.

"No, I don't care for your new hairdo." That may be the truth, but as we said telling the truth is easy, the consequences may be hard. A good solid relationship is based on honesty, trust and self-confidence on the part of both parties. ("Sorry you don't like my hair. I love it. Thanks for your input.")

For a relationship to work among two or more people, the trust must be mutual. To trust others means to have confidence in their honesty, integrity and ethics. Trust is not easy to maintain under the best of circumstances, but what if this person we're looking to trust, to develop a relationship with is... well...different?

Diversity

Logic tells us that as technology unleashes the spread of information all over the globe, the ideas of a middle-aged, white guy in Des Moines, Iowa might not hold the same influence, even in Des Moines, as they once did.

We must be open to the fact that the way we did things in the past may not necessarily be the best way to do them in the future. And the answer to how we should operate in the future may well lie with someone not of our generation or race, who does not speak our language or use the same washroom we use.

In the words of the song, "Colors of the Wind," from the movie, *Pocahontas,* "If you walk in the footsteps of a stranger, you learn things you never knew you never knew." (If animated characters are so smart, can we be far behind?)

Even forgetting all the moral, ethical and honorable issues, being open to the ideas of, and developing a relationship with, people who are "not like us" makes plain old common sense from a selfish standpoint. If we keep doing what we're doing, we'll keep getting what we got; and if we don't want what we "got," we need to do something different. Who best to get something different from than somebody who's different?

Fear of the outlander

Just because technology is advancing at mach speed doesn't necessarily mean we humans are. Through millions of years of evolution, the overly trusting found themselves dead before their time. Therefore in developing a beneficial relationship, "fear of the outlander" is a genuine barrier to be overcome. And with the vitality divergent ideas can bring to us and to our organizations, we better figure how to overcome this fear.

Diversity doesn't mean we must have an office that looks like the United Nations' cafeteria. But we must have diverse ideas, and diverse ideas tend to come from people with diverse backgrounds.

Since those with the same background you have will generally have the same ideas you have, in a knowledge-based environment, one of you isn't necessary.

Developing a relationship with those folks whose ideas are diverse from our own is hard for two reasons:

1) We're attempting to negotiate our way through deep-seated human beliefs – always a risky undertaking.

2) Just when organizations want us to do more with less, act empowered, work together as highly cohesive teams and get results pronto, they tell us to work with people who view the world differently than we do. Notice a potential problem?

A phobe to a phile

To work within the Rule of Relationship, converting a xenophobe to a xenophile isn't necessary. (Now while the type A's are running off to get their dictionaries, let me briefly explain, a "phobe" hates strangers or foreigners, and a "phile" is attracted to them.) People who are like each other tend to like each other, but you don't have to like people to work with them.

Liking the people with whom we work helps, but the key to the relationship is mutual benefit.

Since those with the same background you have will generally have the same ideas you have, in a knowledge-based environment, one of you isn't necessary.

For our purposes here, as crude as it may sound, our bodies are merely a life support system for tomorrow's means of production — the human mind. What color or gender one's body is, the country in which it was born or with whom it sleeps really doesn't matter.

Advancing technology may do more to enhance certain relationships by nullifying these inconsequential external differences we've been fighting and agonizing over during our lifetime than any social programs of the last 100 years.

OTHERS' VIEWS ON RELATIONSHIP

☒ The following story is from *Hearts That We Broke Long Ago* by Merele Shaine:

> And the Lord said to the Rabbi, " Come, I will show you Hell."
>
> They entered a room where a group of people sat around a hugh pot of stew. Everyone was famished and desperate. Each held a spoon that reached the pot but had a handle so long that it could not be used to reach their mouths. The suffering was terrible.
>
> "Come, now I will show you heaven," the Lord said after a while.
>
> They entered another room, identical to the first — the pot of stew, the group of people, the same long spoons. But, there, everyone was happy and nourished.
>
> "I don't understand," said the Rabbi. "Why are they happy here when they were miserable in the other room, and everything looks the same?"
>
> The Lord smiled, "Ah, but don't you see? Here they have learned to feed each other."

☒ Arthur Schopenhauer wrote:

> On a cold winter's day, a group of porcupines huddled together to stay warm and keep from freezing. But soon they felt one another's quills and moved apart. When the need for warmth brought them closer together again, their quills again forced them apart. They were driven back and forth at the mercy of their discomfort until they found the distance from one another that provided the maximum of warm and the minimum of pain.
>
> In human beings, the emptiness and monotony of the isolated self produces a need for society. This brings people together, but their many offensive qualities and intolerable faults drive them apart again. The optimum distance that they finally find and that permits them to

> coexist is embodied in politeness and good manners. Because of this distance between us, we can only partly satisfy our need for warmth, but at the same time, we are spared the stab of one another's quills.

☒ In her book, *Thick Face, Black Heart,* author Chin-Ning Chu tells the following story.

> As a young man passed through a forest, he saw a lion taking a piece of meat to an injured tiger. The young man thought to himself, "God is good; He provides for all His creatures. Just look at that tiger — God also takes care of him. As I am the child of God, for certain, God will provide for me."
>
> The young man went back to his small hut at the edge of the forest. He stopped hunting and waited for God to provide for him. A week passed and nothing happened, so he went hungry. Two weeks, then three weeks passed, and still nothing. Soon he was dying of starvation. A holy man passed his hut and asked him what happened. With the little strength left in his body, he told his story.
>
> The holy man said, "When you saw the two animals, you should have learned from the lion and not the tiger. The lion provides for himself and also provides for others."

☒ John Prine, singer and songwriter, uses the line, "Til you said something neither of us knew," to comment on the synergy in relating with another human being.

☒ Carl Jung, the Swiss psychiatrist, defined the term "individuation" in the process of human development as one of becoming fully individual — using what gifts or talents we are given to develop ourselves as fully as possible. Jung is discussing an independent person, but paradoxically we need others to be independent. Knowledge of other's experiences is part of the "gifts or talents we are given" to develop into fully functioning independent human beings.

☒ A quote from a Robert Heinlein novel reads: "A dying culture invariably exhibits personal rudeness. Lack of consideration for others in minor matters. A loss of politeness, of gentle manners, is more significant than is a riot." Maybe that's because if we don't choose to do what's easy to keep a relationship going, how can we ever expect to do the tough stuff? No easy, no tough, no relationship!

REALITY OF RELATIONSHIP

Technology, cost of real estate, bottom-line orientation, environmental and crime issues are prying us away from the daily interactions with other human beings and placing us unceremoniously into our own little isolated world.

How will we relate to others when we may not be obliged to gather together on a daily basis?

Remaining human

I feel very strongly about the quote by Abraham Heschel used on the opening page of the Rule of Relationship:

> Our concern is not how to worship in the catacombs,
> but how to remain human in the skyscrapers.

The concept of remaining human in today's skyscrapers is still valid. We've just moved past and out of the skyscrapers, ironically enough due to technology, back into the equivalent of the "catacombs."

Maybe an updated version could be:

> Our concern is not how to worship
> the technology of the skyscrapers,
> but how to remain human in the catacombs.

The reality of maintaining desired relationships is difficult because:

◆ We're disconnecting physically from each other. Not that we can't maintain a certain level of relationships in Cyberspace; (and maybe some relationships are best to remain there) it's just harder to preserve trusted relationships with the disembodied.

◆ Relationships involve the right touch of honesty, and as I'm sure we've all discovered, much to our amazement, the consequence of honesty is not necessarily the heartfelt thanks of the person with whom we are being honest.

◆ Business relationships are tenuous at best, not knowing if our coworker will be employed tomorrow, or if she is, will her employment come at the expense of our employment?

◆ Personal relationships are generally maintained at a deeper level than strictly business relationships. They therefore require more of what it's tough to give: time and emotional commitment.

Mutual or nothing

Do we form a relationship based on what others can do for us or on what we can do for them? I say neither. The reality is either one would be a long-term loser. Relationships are based on what we can do for each other.

Does that mean if I can do something for others and they can't do something for me, I should dump them? Yes.

I know that sounds self-centered, but let's look at the reality of a one-sided relationship. If it's not mutual, it won't last. It will die a long, slow, agonizing death. Might as well put it out of its misery now! In tomorrow's world of work, both parties will have too many exciting, challenging and purposeful things to do to waste valuable time on a terminal relationship.

Does that mean if I can do something for others and they can't do something for me, I should dump them? Yes.

A strong word of warning:

Since there's such strength in relationships, first be sure there isn't a mutual benefit to a current or desired relationship before you trash it. And it would be very difficult to think of someone who could bring absolutely nothing beneficial to a relationship.

Maybe you just feel good when you're together. You make each other laugh. Maybe your deceased mother would like it if you kept in contact with Aunt Tillie, and following your mother's wishes makes you feel good. You listen to each other. For whatever reason, if the positives of the relationship are mutual, the relationship is worth nurturing.

Look for the connectedness.

> **Before you throw water over the embers of a relationship, be sure you don't need the warmth.**

To paraphrase Walt Disney, "Everybody I have ever met knows something that I don't know." Some of what others know I may need to know to maximize my potential. Without taking a shot at the relationship, I may lose that knowledge forever.

Before you throw water over the embers of a relationship, be sure you don't need the warmth.

SO WHERE DO WE GO FOR RELATIONSHIP?

We need to go inside — the same place we went for Purpose, Confidence and Responsibility.

Funeral invitation list

↳In the Rule of Purpose, I mentioned a job I once had that allowed me considerable free time. To give you an idea of just how much free time I had, while feeling perfectly healthy I compiled a list of everybody I'd like to have come to my funeral.

If this morbid project interests you, don't scrap it because it seems too imposing. Composing a list of those folks you would hope remember you favorably after you're downsized for the final time sounds more complex than it is. The secret is, don't eat the elephant whole.

To get your inventory of the many people with whom you have interacted, hobnobbed, mingled and socialized over the years, bite off life chunks, i.e. the old neighborhood, different levels of schooling, work, bridge groups, etc. (And pledge a dollar to your favorite charity for every time you say "I wonder what ever happened to....")

Creating a funeral invitation list may seem not only a curious thing to do but also like a monumental waste of valuable time to someone who can't find a moment to read a condensed version of *The One Minute Manager.*

But picture if you split your life open and shook it, what would fall out — people.

You'd find all of the people that helped mold you into what you are today. Some worked with a polishing rag and others with a sledgehammer, but without those past relationships today you would be someone else.

But picture if you split your life open and shook it, what would fall out— people.

Analyze that list. Why did you put those specific people on the list? What did you bring to those relationships; what did they bring to you? Do you still maintain any of those relationships? If yes, why? If not, why? Do you miss them? What could you do to reestablish any of these relationships, if that's what you want to do? And a very important question, what are you doing today for your existing relationships that would cause them to choose to come to your funeral?

Looking to the past, what have you learned for the future of your relationships? What relationships would you like to develop in the next year and what are you doing today to make that happen?

Easy getting harder

I'm sitting here listening to a song by country/folk singer, Iris DeMent, entitled, "Easy's Gettin' Harder Every Day." I think that might be the way it is with establishing solid relationships in today's confused, frantic, electrifying times. Here's a list of some ideas which are "easy," but we often choose to make them "harder."

↬ Be sure your work calendar includes the birthdays, anniversaries and special occasions of those who are important to you. Make a short telephone call (ever had somebody sing happy birthday to you on your voice mail?); stop by their home or office; jot a brief note. One of the best relationship time investments we can make! So little time, so much return!

↬Call a standing ovation for a teammate who pushed his or her limit and didn't know anybody noticed, much less cared.

↬Listen, really listen to another human being who needs to be listened to. Put away the papers; turn away from the keyboard. We all know the listening drill. If you're not sure of the importance of the simple act of listening, think back to the last time you were really listened to — an almost religious experience. And we can give that feeling to anybody at anytime, if we choose.

↬Let people know when they impress you. The exceptional waitress, the neighbor who planted a new garden, the desk clerk at the hotel, the janitor who keeps your office space cleaner than you do, the CEO (yes, he or she needs recognition too) who effectively handled a particularly rough restructuring issue. Don't forget what's right under your nose. Note the spouse who vacuumed out of turn, the children who emptied the garbage without being told. Look around; people using extra effort are everywhere.

↬Volunteer. Meet that need for giving back and present yourself with the occasion to interact with people with potentially diverse ideas while serving those who in some way could use your help.

Jeremy Rifkin in his book, *The End of Work*, refers to volunteerism as The Third Sector. Charles Handy in his *Age of Unreason* calls the unpaid work we do, Gift Work. Regardless of the name, the relationship of working with others on a voluntary basis and the understanding and knowledge that unique relationship creates will play an ever more important role in tomorrow's success.

↬Remember people's names. I did business with the same printer for over four years, never getting competitive bids, because the second time I ordered from them, three months after the first order, they called me by name when I walked into the shop. Ego over finances!

↬Practice not so common, common courtesy. "Carl" people and for gosh sake, return telephone calls within 24 hours!

A cemetery full

Give some thought to this opinion.

Any relationships we let die because we're too busy is our choice, but we must be real sure that what we're busy doing is worth the relationship. All too often in today's hectic, unsure environment, we find ourselves putting certain relationships on the back burner and devoting a major hunk of our waking hours to accomplishing the bottom-line goals of an organization. Keep in mind that, for its good, the organization could and would ditch us in a blink of an eye.

Maybe we don't care about the organization's bottom line, or we work for ourselves. We may believe that by putting relationships off until we've made enough money or status to satisfy our ego or perceived needs, we can pick up the relationship later at a more mutually beneficial time. The cemetery is full of skulls that carried around that thought. Call an old friend, make a new one — now.

For more thoughts on relationship, in addition to the books already mentioned, consider reading: *The Soul of a Business* by Tom Chappel (Bantam), *The Personal Touch* by Terrie Williams (Warner Books), *A Peacock in the Land of Penguins* by B. J. Hateley and Warren Schmidt (Barrett-Koehler).

RELATIONSHIP: The short version

FutureWork thinking brings us a new playing field. Each of us has as good a chance at success as anyone else if we utilize the Rules to maximize our talents. Since all of us together have more knowledge than each of us alone, to maximize our individual and collective talents, sharing our skills and abilities makes good sense.

To be thrilled about sharing, we must understand relationship as a Rule for **FutureWork** is not built on the law of scarcity (there's only so much work so I'd better hoard mine), but on the law of abundance (work creates work and there will be plenty for us all).

Our philosophy must be, "If your end of the boat goes down, so does mine." Together we row merrily down the stream.

FutureWork:
Five Rules for a New Game

RULE 1 - PURPOSE

RULE 2- CONFIDENCE

RULE 3 - RESPONSIBILITY

RULE 4 RELATIONSHIP

RULE 5 - FUN 

Enjoy the little things
for one day you may look back and realize
they were the big things.

Robert Brault

RULE 5

ENJOY THE TRIP

FUN

***Fun is the knowledge
that everything is OK
in our world.***

TEX IS DEAD

Tex died yesterday. I doubt any of you knew Tex. I didn't, and I was his next-door neighbor for more than two years. You know how it is. Both of us working, doing our "thing," just "takin' care of business." Tex was a manager at an automobile dealership, and the goings and comings from his 12-hour-a-day, six-day-a-week dedication was all of Tex I knew.

You may be different, but when anybody I know dies, my brain begins to rearrange priorities, seemingly against my will. I start talking to myself more than usual using phrases like, "In the grand scheme of things," and then desperately try to figure out what the heck is "the grand scheme of things."

Tex knew for about six months that he was dying. I wonder if during those months he ever felt angry or frustrated over the car deals he was unable to pull off during his years of hard work or over the weeds filing for permanent residency in his lawn?

I wonder whether he worried about the potential sale of the car dealership. I wonder if he concerned himself over what his boss thought of him or what his neighbors thought of him. I wonder if he stayed awake at night considering his new advertising campaign or his receding hairline. But most importantly...

I wonder if Tex had fun.

FUN: What is it and why is it a Rule?

Fun differs from the other Rules in that once you have chosen your purpose, painted your vision, assessed reality, developed confidence, embraced the benefits of failure, taken risks, exuded self-esteem, assumed responsibility for your life, maintained control, communicated honestly, been trustworthy, appreciated diversity and maintained appropriate relationships, you automatically get — fun.

Fun doesn't mean we run around all day like Bozo the Clown. Having fun doesn't mean drawing happy faces ☺ ☺ ☺ on all of our correspondence or saying, "Have a nice day!" until the gag reflexes of those around us kick in.

Fun is an inner contentment.

Fun feelings range from tranquil and calm to giddy and joyful. Fun is the knowledge that everything is OK in our world. Fun is not seeing the glass as half empty or half full, but seeing a glass that's twice as big as it needs to be (thanks, George Carlin). Fun is a smirk.

Fun is enjoying the trip.

REFLECTIONS ON FUN

The trip — ah! delicious

The trip is a series of present moments.

Those moments in the instant they're lived become our past. The instant before they're lived, they're our future. The trip is right now.

Think about how much fun we forfeit in the present by focusing on what might happen in the future or what did happen in the past. And as a by-product of a past/future focus, we destroy the present.

As a child I remember one Norman Rockwellian July 4th celebration complete with hot dogs, soda pop, potato chips, ice cream, family, the American Flag and enough fireworks to blow the fingers off of every kid there. Sounds like first-class fun, eh? But the entire time we were "celebrating," I was fretting about having to go to swimming lessons the next day, and I hated swimming lessons. So, I blew a potentially memorable present moment by focusing on an undesired future event. I was not enjoying the trip.

The question we need to ask ourselves is, "How are things right now?" During the 4th of July celebration, everything was great for me. Why would I ruin a perfectly good moment dwelling on something that hadn't happen yet?

Of course I was only a child; adults know better, don't they?

As workers in this evolving world of work, how often do we ruin a perfectly good present moment over some organizational change that's rumored to be occurring in six months — maybe.

What about focusing on how are things right now? Am I healthy? Am I secure today? Is my stomach full? Is my family happy? Disregard what's happened in the past or what we're projecting will happen in the future, right now, this moment, am I having fun?

Stop fertilizing last year's flowers.

Here is how Tom Crumb depicts enjoying the trip in his book, *The Magic of Conflict*:

> The samurai is being chased by a bear. He literally runs off a cliff. As he's falling, he grabs a branch.
>
> He looks up and sees the bear leaning over the cliff, clawing at his head, missing only by inches. As he looks down to the ground below, only about fifteen feet, he sees a lion leaping up, missing his feet only by inches. As he looks at the branch he is clutching, he sees two groundhogs gnawing away at it. He watches as his lifeline disappears, bite by bite.
>
> As he takes a deep, long breath, he notices, next to his branch a clump of wild strawberries. In the midst of the clump is a great, red, juicy strawberry. With his one free hand, he reaches over, picks the strawberry, puts it in his mouth, chews it slowly and says, "Ah! — delicious."

The samurai was responsible to some degree for the bears of his past, lions of his future and the reality of the groundhogs, but as far as what he makes of the trip, the present moment, the fun, the strawberry, "Ah! — delicious."

If what we're doing is not "delicious," why are we doing it?

If what we're doing is not "delicious," why are we doing it? As Nietzsche said, "Is not life a hundred times too short for us to bore ourselves?"

A whole lot a shakin' going on

The 1994 California quake was the lead story on the morning news. Our attention was captured, (actually the story grabbed our attention by the throat) because our son, Dave, was staying in Hollywood a few miles from Northridge, but not enough miles away for his mother and me.

After several attempts to call his apartment, we finally got through. His roommate told us Dave had spent the night at a friend's apartment in, where else, Northridge.

We set a family record watching TV news. CNN's feature story concerned the epicenter of the quake which was within a stone's throw of a Northridge apartment building. Because there were deaths, they did not release the names of the casualties or, rightfully so, the address of the apartment.

There we sat, our fun melting all over the couch. We were destroying a present moment over concerns about what might have happened. Then the craziness of our thoughts hit us. If they had announced that some person in an apartment in Northridge, California won the $40 million lottery, would we be out now celebrating Dave's good luck?

Why were we so quick to jump to the negative, thus spoiling the present moment? Wouldn't greeting the news in a neutral way have been most appropriate?

The question we should have been asking was "How is Dave to the best of our knowledge right at this moment?" The answer was, "The same as he was just before we heard the first newscast."

Yeah, but what if...?

When they announce a restructuring that will affect 10% of the work force, do we see ourselves in the affected 10% or the unaffected 90%? How does that view influence our fun?

Yeah, but what if...?

"What if...?" is a two-edged sword. If we ask "What if...? (what if I'm in the affected 10%) and don't really mean it as a question but actually as a statement of truth, our insides act accordingly.

Scratch off one fun moment.

If our "What if..?" is asked in a planning mode, "What if I'm in the affected 10%? OK, I'll make some calls to folks I've been networking with, update my résumé and take a couple more credits towards my degree." Now we're experiencing a challenging, exciting, eventful present moment.

Vertical coffins

One of the dictionary definitions of fun is: playfulness.

Are we playing with life or working at it?

Charles Garfield in his book, *Peak Performers*, tells a story of playfulness. The story is about a toll booth collector Garfield met on a trip across the Oakland-San Francisco Bay Bridge. The booth was rocking. This man had music playing loudly, and he was dancing up a storm. The toll booth looked and sounded like a one-person rock concert. Garfield got to talk to the collector later, and his story is a good example of playfulness, of someone enjoying the trip.

> **Are we playing with life or working at it?**

The toll collector said he was going to be a dancer someday, and he believed he had the best job in the world. He explained, "I don't know why anyone would think my job is boring. I have a corner office, glass on all sides. I can see the Golden Gate, San Francisco, The Berkeley Hills. Half the western world vacations here...and I just stroll in every day and practice dancing... and my bosses are paying for my training."

Here was a man having fun.

This collector couldn't understand how the other collectors could spend eight hours a day in what he described as "vertical coffins" when with a little change in point of view and a dash of imagination they could go from a job they may have thought of as dull, tedious and boring to one that's amusing, entertaining and exciting.

Toll takers not enjoying the trip, ironic, eh?

A major component in the success of any trip is how thoroughly we've packed. In our metaphorical life trip, we should check our baggage to be sure we have an adequate supply of balance and quality, wrapped tightly in a big old sense of humor. Then we'll be able to balance what's important in our quality life and have a laugh or two along the way.

COMPONENTS OF FUN

Life Balance

If we live to be 74 years of age, we will have had approximately 648,684 hours to balance. I personally do not believe that life has to be, nor can possibly be, uniformly balanced among all the following aspects of the human existence:

Spiritual	Family
Social	Financial
Emotional	Physical
Intellectual	

Life balance must be more like another of *Webster's New World Dictionary* definitions of balance: *pleasing harmony of various elements...; harmonious proportions as in a painting.* What is considered a "harmonious proportion" for one is not considered the same for another. The proportions of the above which we determine pleasing for ourselves depend on Rule 1, Purpose.

The choice of how our life is balanced will be made. If we don't make the choice, then something else will!

The all-leather, NFL regulation football inscribed — *1963 Chicago Bears*

The year was 1964. The place Chicago. A man with whom I worked had acquired a couple of special all-leather, NFL regulation footballs, inscribed — *1963 Chicago Bears*, and was selling them at a good price.

I knew my first son was on the way. (That was pre-ultra sound, but we figured we had a 50/50 chance to have a son.) It was a chance

I was willing to take. I bought the football. I now had my son Tom's "coming home from the hospital" gift, an all-leather, NFL regulation football, inscribed — *1963 Chicago Bears*. That was something special.

When Tom was about five or six years old, he was rummaging around in the garage as only that age can rummage, and he came across the special all-leather, NFL regulation football, inscribed — *1963 Chicago Bears*, and asked if he could play with it.

I explained to him, with as much logic as I felt he could understand, that he was still a bit too young to play carefully with an all-leather, NFL regulation football, inscribed — *1963 Chicago Bears*. It was special.

We had that conversation a couple of more times in the next few months and soon the requests faded away.

That next fall, after watching a football game on television, he said, "Dad, remember that football you have in the garage? Can I use it to play with the guys now?" With eyes rolling up in my head I replied, "Tom, you don't understand, you just don't go out and casually throw around an all-leather, NFL regulation football, inscribed — *1963 Chicago Bears*. I told you before; it's special."

Well, he stopped asking altogether, but he did remember, and a few years later he told his younger brother, Dave, about the all-leather, NFL regulation football, inscribed — *1963 Chicago Bears* that was special and kept somewhere in the garage. So Dave came to me one day and asked if he couldn't take that special football and throw it around for awhile.

It seemed like I'd been through this before, but I again patiently explained that you just don't go out for no reason, and throw around an all-leather, NFL regulation football, inscribed — *1963 Chicago Bears*. Soon he stopped asking. That was more than 16 years ago now.

A couple of months ago I was in the garage looking for some WD-40 (which, with the aid of a rubber hammer, I use to fix about everything I choose to fix) and I noticed a large box that had written across it "coveralls."

I couldn't remember bringing along any coveralls when we moved from Chicago to Albuquerque, so I opened it up and there was the all-leather, NFL regulation football, inscribed — *1963 Chicago Bears*.

You know what? It wasn't very special anymore. No, it wasn't very special at all.

I stood alone in the garage, the boys had long since moved away from home, and I realized the all-leather, NFL regulation football, inscribed — *1963 Chicago Bears*, never was special. Children playing with it when it was their time was special. I had blown those precious present moments never to have again, and I had saved a hunk of leather filled with air. For what?

I took the football across the street and gave it to a family with young kids. A couple of hours later I looked out the window, and the kids were throwing, catching, kicking and letting skid across the cement my all-leather, NFL regulation football, inscribed — *1963 Chicago Bears*. Now it was special!

That experience gave me a good insight into how I was balancing my life. How much importance I was giving to having "things!"

How many of us are putting our lives out of balance by applying so much significance to the financial aspects of our lives? How many of us are "doing more with less," "doing better faster," and "sticking 12 hours of work in a ten-hour bag," to insure we have "things" (and then don't appreciate what we have)?

Are we working for dishes that are too good to eat off of, furniture that's too good to sit on, clothes and expensive bottles of wine for the particular occasion that never comes, while at the same time letting the one-of-a-kind, never-to-be-repeated moments — the fun in life — get away?

Ex Tex and the balance of life

The bumper sticker referred to in the Rule of Purpose read, "The main thing is to keep the main thing the main thing." The "main thing" and "the grand scheme" mentioned in telling about my late neighbor Tex, both boil down to one word — priorities.

Priorities are formed by knowing our purpose. Establishing our priorities allows us to rank the various aspects of our lives, i.e. establish "harmonious proportions" to develop balance.

Balance is how we allocate our time.

Tex had access to all the time he will ever have in this life. Time, other than being nature's way of keeping everything from happening at once, is our prime commodity as human beings.

We don't waste time or save time; all we can do with time is spend it. Are we spending our time because it's there to spend, or are we spending it to accomplish our purpose?

The balance in our lives, the proportions we blend into our "life's

Are we spending our time because it's there to spend, or are we spending it to accomplish our purpose?

stew," will not (and maybe should not) remain the same. If our purpose is not being met, or if we feel we can accomplish our purpose in a more efficient manner, we must be free to readjust our balance.

It's only natural that ex-Tex's balance was readjusted when he knew his life was coming to an end. My guess is that sunsets and sunrises looked even more spectacular to Tex as his "days dwindled down to a precious few." Also good bet would be to say that spending time with the family, going to church, grilling chicken on the Weber for fajitas and even cutting the grass, outranked his desire for the success of the car dealership.

Six-six or sixty

Most of us don't know how much time we have left to balance. Six months, six years, or 60 years?

But as long as we remain on the alive side of the "alive/dead" scale, we have 168 hours per week to balance. If you're like most of us, you have all 168 filled with various activities. (If you find yourself with absolutely nothing to do for an hour each day, please skip to the next section.) Given that each of us have our days filled with either urgent and/or important things to do, when something new to do enters the picture, where do we find the time to do it?

Peter Drucker said, "It's not so much knowing how to grow or change as it is knowing what to abandon." We find time by abandoning something we're now doing. Does what we're choosing to abandon affect our balance?

Having fun when our lives are out of balance is hard. Knowing and acting on the "main thing" keeps our lives in balance.

Quality of Life

Like beauty, success, and risk taking, quality is in the eyes of the beholder. We know when we have quality of life, and we know when we don't.

We can't let others judge our quality of life nor, as tempting as it may be, should we judge the quality of others' lives.

The quality of life question to ask for success in **FutureWork** is, "Does life contain the proper ingredients for enjoying the trip?" If not, maybe through a fuzzy purpose definition, a lack of confidence, choosing not to take responsibility or declining to absorb the energy of others, we're choosing not to maximize the quality of our lives.

We first determine what quality means for us, what we may be missing to make quality happen, and then go get it.

Zig-zag

Often we read in the newspapers or know of someone with difficult physical or mental challenges who still seems to be, to our utter amazement, having fun. Also there are people who, hang on to your hats for this one, have actually LOST THEIR JOBS and are still having fun!

The events in our lives don't determine the quality of our lives, our reactions to those events do.

Granted, the trip is not always smooth. If you were to look at a diagram of mountain climbers going from the base camp to the mountain top, you can bet the path they travel would not be straight. They will zig-zag their way to the top. The trip would seem to be quicker and easier if they walked a straight line, but the terrain doesn't always allow quick and easy.

> **The events in our lives don't determine the quality of our lives, our reactions to those events do.**

The terrain on our life's trip isn't always a straight line either. The trip to our "mountain top" depends on how many rocks, boulders and rivers are in our way, but we need to remember the number and immensity of the obstacles do not have to mar the beauty of the trip. Might rocks, boulders and rivers actually enhance the quality of the trip?

The obstacles and solutions to a quality life do not have to be humongous. They can be of the everyday variety. For example:

Shoulds, multitudes and machetes

Barney, an old buddy, came to my motel room to join me in sipping a grown-up's refreshment. I was glad this room belonged to the motel and I was just renting for a couple of nights because the room was not "user friendly." The chair wasn't near the light; the couch wasn't convenient for watching TV. But it was the motel's room, and they set it up this way so I put up with it.

Barney didn't.

He walked into the room, wet down his ice cubes, sat in the chair and said, "This is no good." He got up moved the chair to the other side of the room, unplugged the lamp, set it next to the chair creating a nice and cozy reading area. Next he rearranged the top of the dresser altering the position of the TV to directly face the couch. I now had a pleasant room. My quality of life in a small way, had improved.

What was the difference between Barney and me? Barney saw the options, assessed current reality, had a vision of a cozy room and took action. I, on the other hand, thought they set the room this way, and that must be the way they wanted it to be.

Today's work environment is "set," but we must be open to the multitude of options in **FutureWork** thinking and be able react to them. Don't look at current work and determine where you'll fit in the future — look at work the way you want work to be and create your fit.

On the other hand, decisions we make that affect our quality of life can be more significant than everyday events.

Ray, another old buddy, worked at five different companies while I did what I "should" do and stayed with one company. I would wonder about Ray because in the '60s and '70s job hopping was just not done. It looked like you couldn't get your act together. All the time I had my act together, my nose to the grindstone and shoulder to the wheel. Ray was expanding his options.

One day Ralph, an acquaintance Ray knew through playing racquetball, approached Ray and asked if he would be interested in coming financially and physically into Ralph's fledgling business. What a silly question! Everybody knows you're not suppose to take chances like that!

Ray didn't.

The business has since been sold. Ray is a millionaire currently living his purpose by working with the Peace Corps in Hungary.

Don't look at current work and determine where you'll fit in the future — look at work the way you want work to be and create your fit.

What was the difference between Ray and me? While I was busy traveling down the path of the multitudes, Ray, with machete in hand, was cutting through the less-traveled path, hacking his way to Hungary.

A quality life is not shoulds and multitudes; it's machetes.

Sense of Humor

Does your joke appreciation run more toward:

Did you know that ancient fishing villages bartered with fish instead of money? They were the first to use credit cods.

or

This morning I woke up to find that everything in my apartment had been stolen and replaced with an exact duplicate.

or

Maybe jokes don't tickle your sense of humor at all. Maybe watching someone fall asleep in a meeting and slide out of his chair is more your style.

Having a sense of humor doesn't mean your body must contort with raucous laughter five times a day, but it does mean you appreciate the humor that's inherent in all situations.

[Laugh Break — *A friend told me that between his boss and all the rumors flying around, he was under so much stress he has migraines, high blood pressure, sleepless nights and an ulcer. He told me he was not sure if he was going to die of a stroke or a heart attack. When I asked him why he stayed with that company, he said, "Because we have a great health plan."*]

A title I considered (for probably longer than I should have) for this book was:

Dismounting the Donkey:
Five Steps for Getting Off Your Ass
in Business and Personal Life.

While that title sums up the Rules we've been discussing, taking into account the sensibilities and the lack of a sense of humor affecting some folks today, it may have said more than I wanted it to say. So I took the concepts and put them into a title which says just what I wanted to say, and can occupy an up-front position on your local bookstore shelf.

When did we get so darn serious?

When do we as humans generally hit our "laugh peak?" I've never read any such study, but if there were a study like that, would you bet the farm on the answer being we laughed more at ten years old or 40 years old?

When I ask people to explain why they might have laughed more when they were younger, their answer usually is something like:

"Sure, things were funnier as a kid because that was before I got responsibilities." What in the heck does that mean?

Does it mean "I have taken the same basic events that have occurred throughout my life and given them a different framework. Now when they occur, I choose to cry rather than laugh?"

I'll buy the truth, not the logic, of that answer.

[Laugh Break — *I was almost thrown out of college during a metaphysics final. I was caught looking into the soul of the guy next to me.* Woody Allen]

Tears from the eyes, milk from the nose

When is the last time you have had a giant, knock-down, drag-out, face-contorting laugh, the kind where tears come out of your eyes, milk comes out of your nose, and you haven't drunk any in more than an hour?

[Laugh Break — *Horses must be deaf because you see so few of them at concerts.* George Burns]

When I started talking to different organizations, one of the first things I noticed was most people were not having fun. They were not enjoying the work life they have chosen to live every day. In a recent study, only three percent of American workers chose Monday as their favorite day. (And they probably had a work week of Wednesday through Sunday.)

When is the last time you have had a giant, knock-down, drag-out, face-contorting laugh, the kind where tears come out of your eyes...?

Remember TGIF and Hump Day. What do these terms tell us about our love of work or our ability to sense humor in a situation? What does it tell us about having fun on the trip?

Look for humor in your workplace because there's an awful lot of funny stuff going on.

While I admit finding humor is easier when something happens to somebody else (and we should take humor where we can get it), but don't pass up the humor potential of looking in the mirror. We don't always have to be so serious. Remember what Lily Tomlin said, "The trouble with the rat race is even if you win you're still a rat."

Look for humor in your workplace because there's an awful lot of funny stuff going on.

[Laugh Break — *The U.S. Congress voted to ban advertisements for snuff and chewing tobacco. A tobacco industry spokesperson attempted to refute those negative charges, but his lips fell off.* Dave Barry]

Stress

Psycho-physiological abnormality

Ready to dampen our fun, detour our trip, dip the balance, and diminish the quality of life while dousing our sense of humor, is our old adversary — stress.

Stress has been described as: Psycho-physiological abnormality at the structure of the chemical level caused by undue pressure of experience.

Is that a bummer, or what?

Since just thinking about that definition could negatively affect our fun, let's see if we can't make the most of stress.

Like most other factors in our lives, stress has a good and a bad side.

Years ago a psychiatrist, Robert Yerkes, formed a theory known as the Yerkes-Dodson Law. The model for the theory which explores the productivity of positive stress and negative stress follows:

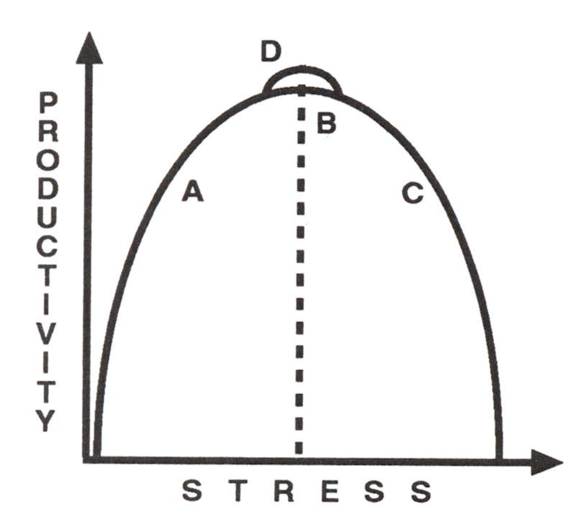

There's a technical, medical word for a total lack of stress. The word is — dead. We need stress just to get up in the morning. This model tells us that the more stress we experience the more productive we become (A) up to a point. At (B) more stress than we can handle occurs; we go into a mental and/or physical meltdown (C).

There is a point in our lives where the maximum pressure produces the maximum output. At point A we are dynamite; we're having fun. We all have a point A. When we are on the A side, we're still in our comfort zone. Life is good. That's positive, productive stress, and there's a word for that. It's called "eustress," the good stress.

When we cross over the line, we are now in the area of negative stress. We are entering our danger zone (C). Point C is called distress/disease/disorder. This negative stress eats away at our fun.

History and logic tell us that certain events in our lives, now and in the future, will not go away just because we want them to go away. Enjoying the trip, by not wasting time and energy fighting events that are out of our control, (and many are even out of our influence) is in our best interest. Better than fighting stress is flowing with stress.

While trying to stop all the stressors in our lives is useless, utilizing the suggestions in the *So Where Do We Go for Fun* section will enable handling just a little more (D) of what life dishes out and maintaining a desired balance and quality of life.

Ducks

Consider the events that we too often let get in the way of our having fun, events that evoke negative stress and, in general, if we choose to let them, ruin the trip for us.

Interruptions, plans not working, unpleasant rumors, or angry internal/ eternal customers — can we legitimately describe these everyday events as catastrophes, tragedies, calamities, disasters, the end of life as we know it?

> **Better than fighting stress is flowing with stress.**

Should we willingly give these commonplace events (over which we have little or no control) the power to stomp all over our fun, to mess with our trip?

A saying applies here, "Seldom are we plagued by lions; more often we suffer the ignominy of being eaten by ducks."

Aren't the events in our lives we judge as negative actually the ducks in our lives? Arrive at work one morning and find a stack of irate customer call-backs — first nibble. Then in the stuffed in-basket appears a memo announcing a policy change — another nibble. At the end of the day, we're drop-kicking pigeons on the way home from work wondering why we're not having fun.

When we wish to add more fun in our lives, we must eliminate those aspects of our lives not meeting the "fun" criteria. But the ducks are here to stay. What we must eliminate is choosing a negative reaction when we find ourselves in the middle of a duck pond.

We'll begin having fun when we reach the point in our lives when we truly understand that these ducks have lives of their own, and they don't give a quack what we think of them!

Certain events in our lives are labeled negative only because we have chosen to label them negative. It's not what they "are," and it's not what they "have to be."

OTHERS' VIEWS ON FUN

☒ Charles Spezzano writes in his book, *What To Do Between Life and Death:*

> You don't really pay for things with money. You pay for them with time. In five years, I'll have put enough away to buy that vacation house we want. Then I'll slow down. That means the house will cost you five years — one-twelfth of your adult life.
>
> Translate the dollar value of the house, car or anything else into time, and then see if it's still worth it...the phrase spending your time is not a metaphor. It's how life works.

☒ "In order to live life freely and happily you must sacrifice boredom, and it's not an easy sacrifice," is a quote from Richard Bach which Jean and I take very seriously, and it is pretty much responsible for getting us from Chicago to Albuquerque.

☒ Deepak Chopra relates in a tape series, *Magical Mind, Magical Body*:

A study by the Massachusetts Health Education and Welfare department concluded that over 50% of people having heart attacks do not have the standard risk factors associated with heart attacks. Two most important factors they exhibited were 1) job dissatisfaction 2) self-happiness rating. (Are you happy?)

Chopra adds, "More people die in our culture on Monday morning at 9 a.m. than any other time of the week. Only humans can accomplish that. No other animal knows the difference between Monday and Tuesday." If a person is enjoying the trip, what IS the difference?

☒ In a Ziggy cartoon, a psychiatrist asked Ziggy as a kid what he wanted to be when he grew up, and Ziggy said, "That's the trouble; as a kid I always wanted to be a kid when I grew up." Here is another Ziggyism: "Today's a gift; that's why we call it the 'present'."

☒ In the movie, *Joe and the Volcano*, Joe says, "Most people are asleep, but the few who are awake will live their lives in a state of constant total amazement."

☒ The following was written in Sanskirt 4500 years ago:

> Look well into this one day, for it and it alone is life. In the brief course of this one day, lie all the verities and realities of your existence; the pride of growth, the glory of actions, the splendor of beauty. Yesterday is only a dream and tomorrow is but a vision. Yet each today, well lived, makes every yesterday a dream of happiness and each tomorrow a vision of hope. Look well, therefore, to this one day for it, and it alone, is life."

☒ Martha, an acquaintance of ours, died a few weeks ago. (I hope she gets to meet Tex and Carl.) Her family said that her big complaint in her last days was that "Dying is boring." Maybe that's as it should be. Dying=boring; living=exciting.

☒ In their book, *Life Balance*, Linda and Richard Eyre tell this all-too-familiar story:

> Imagine a career woman, upwardly mobile, assertive, much of her identity wrapped up in her position in the firm, home now but still in her business suit. With her briefcase open on the kitchen table, appointment book in hand, she is trying to finish up some calls she didn't have time for at the office. She has been interrupted now several times by her four-year-old son, a round-faced, little boy with big, blue eyes.
>
> "Mom...What's in that big book?"
>
> "This is mommy's appointment book, Timmy. What's in it are important things I have to do and the names of important people. Now, run upstairs and play with your toys."
>
> Timmy wanders towards the stairway looking dejected. Then his face brightens and he turns back to his mom, tugs on her skirt. She looks down on him and says through clenched teeth, "What is it, Timmy?"
>
> "I just wondered, Mommy." Timmy's words are slow, his eyes pleading. "Is my name...in your book?"

Who or what is important enough in our lives to be in our "book?"

REALITY OF FUN

They say a Stradivarius violin's sound diminishes if not played every day. I wonder if the same is true for us?

Are we there yet?

Can we be expected to have fun all the time? Reality is even if we don't lose faith every once in awhile, somebody else will always be ready to dump on us.

Don't let them do it.

Don't choose to put up with those people who are awfulizing and catastrophizing, those people who are forever reading off the "whine" list.

These sourpusses create an environment in which choosing to be "up" is difficult. Enjoying the trip is tough while putting up with constant moaning. The complainers are like adult versions of the kids on a trip yelling, "Are we there yet?"

You may feel that people always use you as a receptacle for complaints. And that may be a reality, but I believe people treat us the way we teach people to treat us. How are we teaching others to treat us?

If I go over to Tanya and start complaining about all the bad things that are going on in my life, she may get down and start shoveling up the muck right along with me. Then I go over to Ramon and start my litany of woe again with him, and he says, "What are you going to do about it?" My reaction would be, "I'm going back to Tanya; I'd much rather snivel and wail with her."

Reality note: To those folks who feel inclined to spill their troubles or problems, remember don't bother telling your friends. Tell your enemies; they'll be glad to hear them.)

Like anything worth having, the reality is we must put energy into our fun. To balance a full life, to upgrade the quality of our lives, and to manage negative stress, all with a sense of humor, take effort. But we can do it if we choose.

SO WHERE DO WE GO FOR FUN?

I know this is getting repetitious, but it's the same place we went for the other four Rules — inside.

How we spend our valuable time is an indication of our priorities, and how we organize our priorities is the balance we have chosen for our lives.

Tests, journals, Mickey Mouse and you

➯Simple test, rank the following 1 through 7 as to the importance you feel they have in your life (1 = the most important). Next rank 1 through 7 according to the amount of time you spend on each (1 = the most time).

	IMPORTANCE	TIME
Spiritual	______	______
Family	______	______
Social	______	______
Financial	______	______
Physical	______	______
Intellectual	______	______
Emotional	______	______

Importance vs. time spent — the discrepancies eat away at our fun.

➯Keep a laugh journal. Write down all the funny things that happen to you each day. Jot a note or two when they happen and go back to your notes in the evening and fill in the particulars. Your cockles will be warmed twice, once when the event occurred and a second time when you think about it.

➯Wear a Mickey Mouse watch. When we look at our watch and see Mickey's smiling face, taking ourselves less seriously is easier. Also the watch is a good trigger to ask ourselves, "Am I having fun yet?"

➯If mice aren't your thing, adopt a cat. They're worth at least a chuckle a day.

↬Keep a picture on your desk of yourself as a child. That little cherub has traveled many a mile. Remember all the good times on the trip, and know more of those times are still available for the choosing.

↬ Ponder some navel-contemplation questions:

⇨ If I had six months to live, how would I change my life?
⇨ Who would I live with if I could live with anyone?
⇨ Where would I live if I had no history of living anywhere?
⇨ What activities would I be engaged in if there were no such thing as money?

Fun is the whole person

↬Fun means the whole person should enjoy the trip. Following are a couple of ways to be mentally and physically fit:

⇨ Exercise

There are 4 theories on why exercise works. They are:

1) Oxygenation — deep breathing by itself is relaxing.
2) Endorphins — exercise stimulates the release of the body's own drugs.
3) Rhythm — rhythm of the exercise itself.

And the biggie —

4) Control — We can exercise how, when, where and for how long we wish.

With this control, for one of the few times in our hectic lives, we're in complete and total charge. Heady stuff!

We have had a weight room at our house for years, but I did little specifically aerobic. The doctor told me running would add years to my life. He was right; after about a month of running, I felt ten years older.

To me running is an unnatural act except running from a crazed animal or to the bathroom. For me in high school and college sports, and then in the military, running was always a punishment. A friend suggested running in place. I said, "Good idea, in place of what?"

Obviously exercise will not work to improve our zest for life if we do not exercise. And we will not exercise over the long term if don't we enjoy it.

So if you feel the same about exercises you have tried as I feel about running, change the exercise — do something you enjoy. The choices of exercises would more than fill up this book.

Juliet Schor, author of *The Overworked American*, said time on the job is growing almost a month a year and the amount of vacation and sick leave is declining by almost four days — we'd better be in shape.

⇨ Meditate

Meditation is a great way to keep us mentally enjoying the trip. A major benefit of meditation is we feel just as relaxed as after exercise, and we don't have to take a shower!

> **The reason many people don't like to spend time alone is they don't like the company.**

When I'm suggesting meditation, I don't necessarily mean staring at a crystal, sitting in the lotus position and chanting a mantra. If that works, fine, but I just mean sitting still for 15 minutes, breathing correctly, deeply and listening to what we have to say to ourselves.

Suggestion: carve out at least 15 minutes a day to just "be." Sit back, breathe deeply and let what happens, happen.

Why would we not want to sit back, relax in solitude and meditate each day? That sounds like something we'd almost pay somebody to let us do. You'd think so, wouldn't you? But as Blaise Pascal, a French philosopher and mathematician, said, "All man's miseries derive from not being able to sit quietly in a room alone." The reason many people don't like to spend time alone is they don't like the company.

When we are alone eyes closed, breathing deeply, our conscious mind disengages. We access our subconscious mind and it goes "Knock, knock! Are you growing and having fun on your job? Are your relationships rewarding and full of mutual satisfaction?" "OK, enough of that," we scream; "Let's turn on the radio."

When I'm in a city like New York or Chicago at rush hour and watch all the people hustling to or from work, about three out of four of them have on headsets. God forbid a battery goes out and they would have to walk all the way to their destinations with only themselves for companionship!

To enjoy our trip to the **FutureWork** state of mind, our transportation must be in good working order, so exercise. (And it's never too late. My mother started running five miles a day when she was 65 years old. She's now 75, and we don't know where the heck she is!) Our transportation must also be reliable under the hood, so meditate for peace of mind.

For more thoughts on having fun, in addition to the books already mentioned, consider reading: *Anatomy of an Illness* by Norman Cousins (Bantam Books), *The Relaxation Response* by Herbert Benson (Avon Books), *Life and How to Survive It*, by Robin Skynner and John Cleese (W.W. Norton), and anything by Dave Barry.

FUN: The short version

Fun is an inner contentment.

Fun feelings range from tranquil and calm to giddy and joyful. Fun is the knowledge that everything is OK in our world. Fun is not seeing the glass as half empty or half full, but seeing a glass that's twice as big as it needs to be (thanks, George Carlin). Fun is a smirk.

Fun is enjoying the trip.

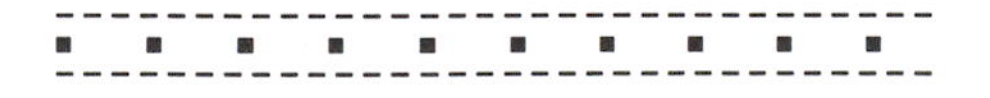

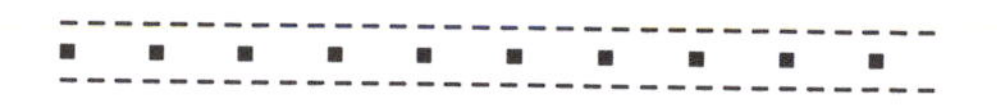

A TICKET TO RIDE

There once was a man who would kneel by his bed each night and say, "Dear God, give me a break and let me win the lottery." After about two months of "Dear God give me a break, let me win the lottery," one night he got on his knees and began his litany, "Dear God give me a break." Before he could finish, from above came a deep, booming voice that implored, "Give me a break and buy a ticket!"

Success in **FutureWork** requires a ticket for the New Game.

Consider the various ways our organizations are preparing for the future. Obviously, the one true path to improved organizational productivity is proving elusive — but the search goes on.

What an exciting time in which to work!

With structures not as yet "set," we are in a most enviable position of being able to fashion our own exhilarating, stimulating and productive tomorrows. But we have to have a ticket to get into the game.

Right now there are people who don't even know us making decisions that will affect our future, making decisions that will change the way we thought our future would be.

Implementing all the Rules with our own ideas and activities or with the ideas and activities in the *So Where Do We Go...* sections of each Rule provides us the choice to live the life we want to live, to be in charge, to be in control.

Maximizing the Five Rules is our ticket for the New Game.

Rule 1 - Know what turns you on - Purpose.

Rule 2 - Be convinced you have what it takes - Confidence.

Rule 3 - Look inside first - Responsibility.

Rule 4 - Remember you're not alone - Relationship.

Rule 5 - Enjoy the trip - Fun.

These Five Rules are natural to us all.

Farms to factories to farms.

Independence to dependence to independence.

We've played the game before, and we can play again.

And now we have the ticket.

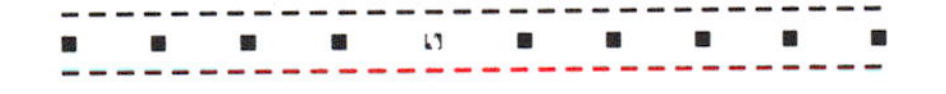

FUTUREWORK:

FIVE RULES FOR A NEW GAME

is dedicated to

and

written for

those men and women

willing to work for their vision

of

an exciting and fulfilling

future.

Acknowledgement

Writing is easy; you just sit in front of the typewriter until blood forms on your forehead.

It's unclear who first wrote that truth, but take away the typewriter and insert a computer, and the author could have been me.

Writing **FutureWork** was a labor, but with "a little help from my friends," it was a labor of love. So I'd like to indulge your patience for two more pages.

The following folks freely gave of their limited time and unlimited insight to the creation of **FutureWork.** I would not feel right closing without acknowledging their significant contributions.

My appreciation:

To the following people – Kerry Boretz, Tomie Casey, Craig Dean, Milt Garrett Ed.D., Billye Gregoire, Vivian Harris, Barbara Howatt, Vickie Hudspeath, Marilyn LeBlanc, Dianne Moody, Maria Petrov, Kay Stanley, Gayle Stewart, Joan Ward Ph.D., Carol Willenbrock and Kirsti Wolfe.

Special gratitude:

To my brother, Bill Payne, who knows more about people in business than anyone I know and to my sister-in-law, Jackie Hertel, for her comprehensive editing work.

To the thousands of workers who have opened their hearts and souls to this traveling observer.

In addition, I feel especially thankful for those who were always there to wipe my bloody forehead, my family...

My parents:

Ardele – A mother I'd wish for everyone. While she had a couple of bad breaks this year, she showed the strength we all knew she had.

Bill – An ethical, honorable, principled and good man. A husband and father with a natural sense of humor. I hope to grow up to be just like him.

My sons:

Dave – Our **FutureWork** model. He knows what he wants and is willing to make the required sacrifices to make it happen.

Tom – A living version of the "lilies of the field." He reveals every day how a person can live and enjoy an "ah! delicious" life. Tom's a strawberry picker.

My best friend, wife, partner, supporter and chief editor:

Jean – The woman who made it all possible, but most important, made it all worthwhile.

NOTES

NOTES

NOTES

FUTUREWORK:
FIVE RULES FOR A NEW GAME

IS AVAILABLE AS A LIVE PRESENTATION.

If you would like to share what you have read, Tom Payne and his staff are available to present to your organization a thought-provoking presentation based on the concepts of **FutureWork**.

Also available are programs based on Tom's previous books, *A Company of One: The Power of Independence in the Workplace* and *From the Inside Out: How to Create and Survive a Culture of Change*, along with other presentations dealing with the human aspects of organizational issues.

LODESTAR programs are available in a variety of interactive formats ranging from keynote addresses to three-day workshops and are designed to meet the specific needs of corporations, professional associations and the general public.

To obtain additional information on LODESTAR, speeches, workshops, and publications or to order copies (quantity discounts available) of *FutureWork: Five Rules for a New Game, A Company of One: The Power of Independence in the Workplace* or *From the Inside Out: How to Create and Survive a Culture of Change*, contact:

LODESTAR★
A Performance Enhancement Company
1200 Lawrence Court NE
Albuquerque, N.M. 87123-1905

800-447-9254 • 505-296-2940 • FAX 505-294-6942